MW01148080

A LITERARY JOURNAL

Flying South #2, 2015

Words Become Pictures

Edited by Robin Chalkley & Anne Civitano

Winston-Salem Writers / Winston-Salem

Winston-Salem Writers
c/o Milton Rhodes Center for the Arts
251 Spruce St.
Winston-Salem, NC 27101
www.wswriters.org

Publisher's Note: This is a work of fiction. Names, characters, places, and incidents are a product of the author's imagination. Locales and public names are sometimes used for atmospheric purposes. Any resemblance to actual people, living or dead, or to businesses, companies, events, institutions, or locales is completely coincidental.

Book Layout © 2015 BookDesignTemplates.com

Flying South #2, 2015/ Robin Chalkley & Anne Civitano, editors. -- 1st ed.
ISBN 978-1-15169159-4-1

"We read five words on the first page of a really good novel and we begin to forget that we are reading printed words on a page; we begin to see images."

—John Gardner, On *Becoming a Novelist*

CONTENTS

{ 1 } From the Editors

Welcome to *Flying South #2, 2015*. We're excited about this issue, and the changes that brought us here. This year we added prize money for the first and second place winners, and received more entries than ever. We got to see writing from all over the South, as well as the rest of the country, and we believe this issue will provide some great reads—the winners' pieces are filled with humor, poetry, art, madness, tenderness and insight. There is painting to be admired, including, from our contributors, more than one Van Gogh reference.

The other big change this year came from our observation of what our Winston-Salem Writers members were writing most. We added a category for novel beginnings (up to 500 words). We were looking for pieces that compelled us to turn the page.

We are happy to announce that all our invited contributors from last year have returned, but with different sorts of pieces.

- Steve Mitchell provided us with his short story, "Garden," in which a couple considers starting their own religion.
- Stan Washburn offered the first chapter of his recent novel, *Van Gogh Only Sold One Painting in his Life, Did You Know That?* It's a fascinating and funny look at the struggles of young artists trying to succeed in the New York City art world.
- Our related video story is a web series of very short films that pose the question, "What if Vincent Van Gogh was somehow dropped into today's Brooklyn, NY?" It was inspired by a photo that went viral on (the website) reddit.

- Carol Roan has shared an email exchange between her children that turned into a hilarious smackdown over punctuation.
- And we're excited to provide our first ever Q&A, this with a pair of writers: award winning playwright and novelist Gordon Dahlquist, and award winning playwright Anne Washburn.

When we gave this issue the theme, "Words Become Pictures," we were thinking of the famous John Gardner quote from *On Becoming a Novelist*, "We read five words on the first page of a really good novel and we begin to forget that we are reading printed words on a page; we begin to see images."

We'd love to hear what you think!

Happy reading,

Robin Chalkley & Anne Civitano
Co-editors, *Flying South #2, 2015*
Winston-Salem, NC
www.wswriters.org

{ 2 } Guest Contributor: Short Story

GARDEN

By Steve Mitchell

They were an unremarkable couple, rooted across from each other in the booth, comfortable in conversation. She, her wheat blonde hair drawn away from her face with a simple clip, her hand resting upon the tabletop. He, broad shoulders against the back of the seat, large hands waving before him in the hidden rhythms of their intimacy. Both were in their late thirties. They talked casually, with a smile and a tilt of the head. They had an ease about them, as if all tension had seeped away, years ago, in the earlier trials of their union. She chuckled at something he said, glancing up as the waiter arrived with dinner, her eyes drifting back toward him with a silent, offhand wink.

The waiter placed plates before them, lingered officiously, then wandered away, losing interest immediately. As soon as he turned his back, their hands slid across the table toward each other, coming together in the center. Their forearms and wrists rested upon the Formica, their fingers clenched, as knotted as a heart. The woman closed her eyes and their heads bowed. From his seat on the far side of the restaurant,

Scott could see the movement of the man's lips. The woman's fluttered too, almost imperceptibly.

"We should start our own religion," Scott declared, returning his gaze to Liza who arrested a forkful of salad centimeters from her mouth, peering up through feathery bangs.

"What?"

"Yeah. Start our own religion. Religions have to begin somewhere, right? Why don't we begin one right now."

The couple at the far table looked up simultaneously, a murmur passing between them. They tightened their hold for an instant before releasing, their hands sliding toward their plates.

"We'll be...oh, I don't know...Anthracites."

"What'll we believe in?"

"We can always work that out later," Scott replied with an offhand wave, "what we need first is a ritual."

Liza rolled her eyes, placing the forkful in her mouth and leaning back against the red leather of the booth. The corner of her mouth turned up in a mocking smile, the tenderness of her gaze warm along his face. She was tall and slender, clad in beige and white; and in that aspect, sloped against the booth, he thought she resembled a gauze parenthesis. She watched him as he began to eat, her bare leg beneath the table settling against his own.

"Would we tell everyone we're Anthracites?"

"Sure, we could say it," he considered, "just not explain it. As if the whole thing were completely self-evident."

"I want an icon."

"And you shall have it. What would you like?"

"A figure we can put on the table between us. We could pray to it. We'll carry it in a linen cloth. Or a velvet bag. We'll remove it tenderly and place it in the center, then we can recite our prayer."

"Shoom dala sheem dala. In lata gilgo."

"Or something like that."

Scott watched the booth across the room intermittently, between conversation and bites of lasagna, while they discussed the possible rituals and vestments of the Anthracitic Church. The other couple laughed, talking easily, completely enshrouded in their attention for each other.

Liza's leg pushed against his own as they talked and he reached down, under the table, to stroke the silk of her knee. The couple across the way now kept their hands to themselves. When he and Liza rose from the booth and moved toward the cashier, the couple remained behind, lingering over dessert.

They went shopping, spending a playful afternoon drifting through shops, examining statuettes earnestly. They studied ballerinas perched with a fragile grace upon single toes. And garish, sad-faced clowns in baggy pants clutching pairs of plaster balloons. They looked at dolphins emerging from crystalline seas and gnarled gnomes with pointed hats and colored orbs. They eased from one counter to another, one shop to another, their fingers occasionally locking together, their hands unconsciously sliding over each other's bodies.

They took up this mission without a thought, as if it had been obvious from the start that they would spend their Saturday afternoon grazing through the downtown arts district in search of just the right figurine upon which one might found a religion. They stopped for ice cream, fully aware that they were searching jointly for inspiration in the mundane, the arrival of grace, an ecstatic epiphany. Neither of them could have said what the figure might look like once discovered and, in fact, they did not discuss the possibilities. Now and then, Liza allowed her fingers to dance over the surface of a delicate object as if its texture might make all the difference. Once or twice, she held a figure in her hand, testing its weight, seeming to consider its potential use as a blunt instrument.

"Here it is!" Liza declared two shops later, and she was right.

It was the figure of a round-faced Aryan boy with a lock of ceramic hair curled neatly in the center of his wide forehead, protruding from beneath a flat, dark derby. His milky skin was smooth and perfect, his fleshy body round and childlike in its rolled plaid shirt and folded over-alls. He held a simple cane fishing pole, its base resting on the ground, the line falling behind him to a pink ceramic fish motionless at his heels, its eyes bulging its mouth open. The boy's expression was not exactly one of joy, more a quiet and confused bemusement. His eyelids were half closed, his rounded mouth upturned in a blurred smile below his delicate nose. He seemed quite unsure as to what he had accomplished.

Liza stepped into a joyous dance, her body sloping backward as she spun upon one foot, bearing the statuette aloft. He watched her turn, not wishing to interrupt her excitement; wanting, rather, to bask in her glow before taking her hand.

The clerk handled the figure with a cheerful solemnity, turning it in her fingers and inspecting it diligently before placing it on the counter and taking his credit card. She seated the figure within a white cushioned box, then an austere black bag. She produced a Statement of Authenticity from a filing cabinet behind her with the gravity and implied responsibility of a Birth Certificate.

Once outside the store, Liza removed the box from the black bag. On the drive back to the apartment, she placed the box lightly upon her thighs, between her hands, as if it held the most stilling secret or the full measure of the world's ills.

She talked about her week at work, the morning the boss was in a bad mood, the customer who would not leave until she had spoken to the Regional-Manager-in-Boulder on the phone. She talked about the swing hanging from the outstretched arm of a tree in her backyard when she was seven; how damp and cool the shade grew in the summer, how blue the sky seemed through the bare branches in the winter. Scott drove, responding quietly with just enough affirmation to keep her talking.

She shifted in the seat, stretching her legs nearly parallel and angling them toward him. She leaned back against the door, her eyes half closed, her fingers resting along the top of the box in her lap. He wanted to reach across the gear panel and touch her; but sometimes it was more gratifying to delay contact, allowing the desire to build as a spiraling tension in his fingers and tongue.

She had already chosen a place for the figurine in their apartment. She would construct a small shrine at the top of the bookcase in the living room with a bowl, some flowers and a bell. Lord Anthracite would rest there when not accompanying them.

And when, later, she flung herself open to him, he was at once exhilarated and terrified. In that moment, there was a choice made and he knew the choice was made, but he didn't know what had been decided. He felt the decision in his chest, a tiny key entering a tiny lock, then turning. He felt the click as the tumblers fell.

And when, later, she flung herself open to him, he lost himself absolutely in the insistence of their touch. He felt himself dissolve into her skin then further, into the bed, into the room. He felt a joy he knew would one day martyr him.

Steve Mitchell's work has been published in Southeast Review, storySouth, the North Carolina Literary Review, and Contrary, among others. He's a winner of the Lorian Hemingway International Short Story Prize. His short story collection, *The Naming of Ghosts,* is published by Press 53. Steve is co-owner of Scuppernong Books in Greensboro.

{ 3 } Guest Contributor: First Chapter

Van Gogh Only Sold One Painting in His Life, Did You Know That?

By Stan Washburn

Chapter 1

On a sunny Tuscan hillside in the year 1277 the immortal Giotto, then an entirely obscure ten-year-old shepherd, happened to be scratching a drawing on a rock when Cenni di Pepo, known as Cimabue, an influential artist of the old school, passing by chance, noticed what he was doing and in that moment recognized his genius. He swept the child off to be an apprentice in his workshop in Florence— the beginning of great things for Giotto.

More recently, in The Big Apple, Nate Ritzo, an ardent young painter, hurries with two of his canvases through the gallery district. Nate heard the Giotto anecdote when he was a student at the Cozens College of Art (that jumble of converted industrial buildings over by the river). The story, if it's to be believed, proves that long shots do happen— an encouraging thought for a young artist. Although it was an unlikely set of circumstances that launched Giotto's career. What if, on that particular morning, Giotto had found no suitable sharp rock to scratch his drawing with, and when Cimabue passed had just been twiddling his thumbs like any other shepherd? What if his drawing had been on the far side of the rock, where Cimabue couldn't see it from the road? Or if he'd passed earlier in the day, before the boy started drawing? — or later, when shadows obscured the scratches? The more Nate thought about it, the longer the odds got. What if the artist as he walked along had been immersed in the play of light and shadow over the gloriously intricate landscape, and hadn't noticed the shepherd boy at all? What if he'd been detained by some business matter, or an attack of gout, or for whatever reason decided to make his journey another day? Giotto might have lived and died a shepherd. Long before the present, time and the passing seasons would have effaced all traces of his work.

Luckily, that's not what happened. The big front windows of the galleries Nate passes are glorious with the wiggly reflections of façades and steps with ornate banisters opposite, and wavery snatches of pale blue sky. But he isn't admiring the reflections, intriguing as they are; he's watching for the dark silhouettes of the dealers and the black-clad, long-legged gallery girls as they move purposefully around the glamorous track-lit spaces, busily building vast fortunes and mighty reputations.

The Hercules Nestor Gallery is just ahead. A bit of Giotto action is unlikely, Nate realizes, but not impossible; Hercules Nestor himself might perfectly well be standing in his doorway, enjoying the ritual of the cigar, the sweet evening air, the delicate light, as Nate approaches. Hercules notices him. Intermittently between parked and passing cars he catches tantalizing glimpses of the canvas facing him. He's looked at a zillion paintings. He has the hard eye. He understands what he sees.

One moment, young man, he calls in his charming accent. I would so much like to see what you have there.

Nate crosses the street and holds up the two canvases. They are spare, semi-abstract images of machines— a drill press and a stump splitter— in reticent chords of warmish, grayish tones. Very personal and eccentric pieces, not at all what's happening now.

For a long, silent quarter of a minute, Hercules scrutinizes. Bring them in, so I can look at them properly, he says. I am not taking on new artists now, but for my education. Which is what dealers always say to give themselves some latitude, but if they weren't at least a little tantalized, all you'd get is the thousand-yard stare and never a word. So it's looking suddenly, scarily good as Nate follows him inside. He points to a space along one wall beneath a row of large, cartoony paintings encrusted with the bodies of small animals. Nate leans his pieces against the wall and silently steps back. Two bombshell black-clad, long-legged gallery girls have crept up behind Hercules and stare, transfixed. One silently mouths Omigod— and O wow! silently mouths the other. Hercules studies, stepping back and forth so he's squarely in front of each piece, tipping his head slightly this way and that, glancing between them, comparing— and finally nods several small but decisive affirmative nods. I'm impressed, he says, turning to Nate.

It all follows from this moment— studio visit, representation, spectacular show, adulatory reviews, skyrocketing prices, eager groupies—

But now Nate is passing the gallery. There's no one in the doorway. Nate can see the head and shoulders of the black-clad, long-legged girl at the desk. She's intent on something in front of her. No one else is visible. No one is watching the street. No one calls out to him.

Okay, so he knew it was unlikely. But what is unlikely is nevertheless in some degree not impossible. You never know. Rembrandt made it when he was in his twenties. Jacob Lawrence was in the Museum of Modern Art when he was Nate's age.

And just around the corner from Hercules Nestor is Teal Jakes. Teal Jakes isn't as fancy as Hercules Nestor, but still plenty fancy for the likes of Nate. The openings at Teal's glimmering space teem with artists you've heard of and peacocking glitterati and eager, loaded collectors. Her discoveries are often, if not invariably, catapulted into hotness. How inexpressibly sweet, thinks Nate in common with every other aspiring painter in New York, to be one of them.

Of course it's true that in Nate's opinion Teal's artists are about novelty rather than substance, flash rather than weight. But he knows perfectly well that in this hard-scrabble world you have to be a little tough-minded, a little flexible; and if, as he comes along the street this evening, Teal happens to be stepping out of a cab, say, and catches a glimpse of the pieces he's carrying, and stops short and says in her famously assured way, Bring those inside where the light is better, he isn't going to tell her not to waste her time— that his work isn't her sort of thing at all— original rather than trendy, contemplative rather than flashy— that it would just make her other artists look puerile by comparison. No, he'll let her look at them. He'll listen to what she might propose. It might be that she's considering a change of direction for her gallery— that the glamorous dreck she shows is just the best she can find. She might be eager for real painting if she came across some.

But Teal doesn't appear. The black-clad girl at the desk is on the phone, eyes down, scribbling on a pad, and doesn't notice him. Nobody hails him.

He's too proud to look back after he's passed, but he's alert for the clatter of high heels on long, hurrying legs, and an urgent, suppliant voice calling, Just a sec! Just a sec!

But no one pursues him.

Not being hailed or pursued is no surprise, of course, but in the ripeness of Nate's yearning the passing of any possibility, however remote, is a disappointment. Not to luck into Giotto's youthful recognition doesn't doom you to failure, but it does mean a longer, harder road. Edward Hopper, the great American realist, didn't sell his first painting until he was forty. Vincent van Gogh, he of the severed ear, also made his first sale when he was forty, and died before making another.

Nate has tried; he's submitted images of his work to stellar, somewhat sub-stellar, and notably sub-stellar places, and never gotten a nibble. That means that he either finds some other line of work, or settles on some even more notably sub-stellar alternative. Which is what he's done. The paintings he's carrying are destined for No Concessions, a gallery in 981, one of those old warehouse buildings that have been converted to galleries. It's there that Nate is to have his first solo show. It's not the space he would have chosen. There are several respectable, albeit notably minor galleries in 981, but No Concessions is more minor yet. It's situated on the top floor at the far end of a serpentine corridor, next to the rest rooms. Nate has been to thinly attended openings there. The only art world heavyweights who come near the place are the ones hurrying around the corner to relieve themselves. If they glance in the doorway it's never more than a glance. So might a distracted Cimabue have trotted past Giotto to get to that clump of bushes yonder.

[Close of Chapter 1]

Washburn, Stan (2015-05-11). Van Gogh Only Sold One Painting In His Life, Did You Know That? (Kindle Locations 14-76). Andy Ross Agency. Kindle Edition.

You can find the rest of this book, and Washburn's others, by typing "Stan Washburn" into Amazon or Smashwords.

Stan Washburn is a painter, printmaker, and, more recently, a writer. His art is in the collections of the Achenbach Foundation, the Brooklyn Museum, the Boston Museum of Fine Arts, the Philadelphia Museum of Art, and the Portland Art Museum, among others. His work is images of things he sees or wishes he could see around him—and inclines to the whimsical and mildly absurd. His writing is similarly based on experience and sympathetic observation.

{ 4 } Guest Contributors: Video Story

Pictures Become Words: The Van Gogh Show

When North Carolina native Robert Reynolds was spotted on the NY subway by a reddit* user, she took a photo and posted this collage, saying something like, "So, I was riding the subway with Vincent Van Gogh today . . ." Within four days, the photo was viewed over two million times and had over four hundred comments. It was picked up by online and TV networks, many of whom interviewed Reynolds.

A group of Reynold's friends, also from North Carolina and all UNC Greensboro grads who now live in NYC (Franny Civitano, Caitlin Davis, Logan Ford, and Chris Raddatz) got together to conceive *The Van*

Gogh Show as a web series. Their website and YouTube channel seek to answer the questions: *What if Vincent Van Gogh rode the subway? What if he got overwhelmed in Trader Joe's, swiped right on Tinder, made latte art, and took selfies just like you and me? What if he lived in Brooklyn?*

> *The Van Gogh Show follows Vincent Van Gogh's daily mis-adventures from the mundane to the absurd, with an emphasis on the absurd.*
>
> *– vangoghshow.com*

*reddit is a popular social media site for news, photos, entertainment and commentary

Check out the Van Gogh Show website at www.vangoghshow.com, where you will find the links to each episode as it is posted, and/or look for The Van Gogh Show on YouTube.

{ 5 } Guest Contributors: Q&A

NY Times bestselling author and playwright **Gordon Dahlquist** and prizewinning playwright **Anne Washburn** answered five questions for us.

1. What is the worst or most ill-advised piece of writing advice you've heard or received? Elaborate.

Gordon Dahlquist	Anne Washburn
While "write what you know" is perfectly sound advice with regard to acquiring authority as a writer - the more deep your experience of a thing, the more deft and full your articulation - I think it's also stunting if taken too literally, especially to the point of autobiography. "What you know" is less a matter of life events than a way of seeing, or thinking, a point of view. It's much more interesting to see these elements used for stories utterly apart from an author's	"Audiences won't understand this." You have to give people credit for smarts.

| own life. Make things up, just do it rigorously, true to your-self. | |

2. As a two-writer household, what advice do you have for the partners of writers?

G.D. I was once told I was cranky when I was writing, because I was always caught up in it ... and then cranky when I *wasn't* writing, because I was always thinking about working, and I'm afraid that may be true. We both understand that dynamic of walking around with part of your head elsewhere, and how much of daily life gets shoved to the side under deadline or immersion. But we also intimately understand the process and can quite often help the other out, whether that means talking through a problem or simply setting down a cup of tea and backing ... quietly ... away.

A.W. It's lovely for the most part, because we both understand what the other is going through and we're both very forgiving when the other is very immersed in a project -- we know just what that fundamental level of distraction *is*. On the other hand, when we're both really cooking on work the Domestic Standard can fall pretty low so I suppose my advice would be -- don't enter into a two-writer relationship unless you have a high tolerance for occasional bouts of deep clutter and weird provisional meal making.

3. As playwrights, you turn words into not only pictures, but physical things, with actors and directors and audiences. At some

point, the project will become collaborative. How does this impact your process? How is playwriting different from other writing? OR What is the best/worst thing about writing for the stage?

| G.D. Playwriting is to novel writing as charcoal is to a palette of colored paints. In playwriting you invoke an entire world out of what people say, knowing that in real life most people don't commonly say things that would define a world - that's taken for granted, because they already know. So it's proceeding through inference and hints, and with a limited vocabulary - since you're only using the words those people, whoever they are, would actually say. Making a play also means writing with explicitly non-verbal elements - with time, especially, and with silence, and also with physical space, knowing how the details of a room inform (how far apart people are standing, for example) what the words might mean - and in that sense is a touch closer to something like music. | A.W. I think when you begin writing plays, commonly, you create something which is much more literary -- in the sense that it's its own discrete piece of writing. The more you make plays and the more you understand the possibilities collaborations open up, the more you start to write play as documents, blueprints -- you still want it to be a strong reflection of your own vision, and you want to provide strong guidance, but you also want to leave a certain amount of opportunity for others to create within the work, because that energy will make the production that much stronger.

The best thing about writing for stage is that the genius of others can make your own genius even more geniusy and the worst is that the non-genius of others can destroy all that you and everyone else is striving to create. |

4. What is your best advice for writers?

G.D. Write every day. It's a process of reverse-erosion.	**A.W.** Write the work you think no one but you will like.

5. Do you have anything to say about gender and writing in general, or writing for the stage?

G.D. There are a number of pretty active public conversations around gender in the book world: women make up a significant majority of book readers and book buyers, yet writing by men is given much more (and more serious) media coverage; genre writing traditionally skewing to men (e.g. mysteries, thrillers, comics) is accepted in mainstream media while genre writing skewing toward women (romance, especially, despite it making up the single largest slice of the American publishing pie) is more or less dismissed. Hopefully readers will keep pushing publishers and the publishing media to take these issues, and others, seriously. This is also an issue in the theatre - there are more productions across the country of male playwrights than female, but in New York,	**A.W.** Oh....not really. I think we pay more attention to men, take them more seriously, by "we" I mean: humans. I can well imagine that I don't get the same regard or attention I would if I were a man and there are studies which show that men are produced out of proportion to their commercial value and I do think it's useful to keep that information somewhere in the foreground of people's attention. At the same time I feel respected in my work with collaborators which is the most important thing to me; I acknowledge that kind of gender disparity as a sort of floating invisible toxin which I try to remember to monitor but it doesn't cause me any anguish in my day to day dealings.

for new writing anyway, things are getting closer to parity. Amongst the people actually running institutions, less so, but that seems like a different track of change, with an even more entrenched resistance.

Gordon Dahlquist is a playwright and novelist. His plays include *Messalina, Delirium Palace*, and *Tomorrow Come Today*, and have been performed in New York, Los Angeles, Dallas, and elsewhere. His first novel, *The Glass Books of the Dream Eaters*, was a *NY Times* bestseller and has been published in 30 countries. His other novels include *The Dark Volume, The Chemickal Marriage*, and *The Different Girl*. He lives in New York.

Anne Washburn's plays include *Mr. Burns, The Internationalist, A Devil At Noon, Apparition, The Communist Dracula Pageant, I Have Loved Strangers, The Ladies, The Small* and a transadaptation of Euripides' *Orestes*. Her work has been produced by 13P, Actors Theater of Louisville, The Almeida, American Repertory Theatre, Cherry Lane Theatre, Clubbed Thumb, The Civilians, Dixon Place, Ensemble Studio Theater, The Folger, The Gate, Playwrights Horizons, Red Eye, Soho Rep, Studio Theater, Two River Theater Company, Vineyard Theater and Woolly Mammoth.

{ 6 } Guest Contributors: Punctuation Geeks

Grammar Duel: An Exchange Among Siblings

By Melissa Roan Naegilin, Christopher Roan, & Tim Roan.
Contributed by Carol Roan

Editor's Note: Carol Roan, mother to Melissa, Chris and Tim, sent an email to her children about a publishing event she had attended.

> *Carol wrote: An editor and I got to talking about semicolons because I love semicolons. "Semicolons and dashes," said the editor. I asked how she felt about ellipses. She's for them. She said she had suggested a semicolon in a sentence to one of her authors. He refused, saying he already had one semi-colon in the book . . ."*

June 10

I was going to use a semicolon today, but wanted to confirm its use. I thought you might find this website interesting:
http://theoatmeal.com/comics/semicolon

23

Chris

June 10

Love it.

Tim

June 13

Damn. I seem to be missing the semicolon chromosome - I prefer dashes and parentheses (when I add asides and descriptions.)

But, I do remember to put the period INSIDE the parenthesis regardless (not irregardless) of how odd it may look sometimes - because that is how I am genetically coded.

On second thought, maybe dashes and parenthetic asides are evolutionarily superior and soon, a la Darwin, all of you semicolon types will become extinct.

One thousand years from now, some archaeologist will unearth documents with an unknown symbol ";" Academia will be torn asunder and many doctoral dissertations will be written about ";"

Love - always (even though I might possibly share some of your defective, and soon to become extinct, semicolon genetic material.)

Melissa

June 13

I thought long and hard about my response. I believe that when they unearth the document they will realize the beauty of the semicolon, wonder at the horror that is the parenthesis, and recoil from the dash.

The mutant colon . . . . semicolon

Chris

June 14

Chris,
It's unfortunate you thought long and hard about your response, mainly due to what you typed after said experience.
Ellipses . . . really?
Bush league.

Melissa - long lost sibling of the north,
I hear ye loudeth and clear on the love (and usefulness) of the dash and parenthetical elaboration.
We are all, it seems, in accord on the matter of grammar and its beauty.

Lastly, shall we not turn our gaze to our simple friend, the comma?

Best,
Tim

June 14

Tim,
What the hell drug are you on? Semicolon meth? "Ye." Really? Is that how they talk in the swanky parts of

Brooklyn nowadays? Are you some kind of commie? In the good old US of A, no self-respecting real American would ever use "Ye."

(Notice the period inside of the quotation mark.) Good old American grammar just like they used when they landed on Omaha Beach. God Bless America!

Love,
Melissa

This message is semicolon free and therefore safe to read.

June 25

Let's hope our little "tiff" doesn't come to this:
NEW YORK—Law enforcement officials confirmed Friday that four more copy editors were killed this week amid ongoing violence between two rival gangs divided by their loyalties to the The Associated Press Stylebook and The Chicago Manual of Style.

"At this time we have reason to believe the killings were gang-related and carried out by adherents of both the AP and Chicago styles, part of a vicious, bloody feud to establish control over the grammar and usage guidelines governing American English," said FBI spokesman Paul Holstein, showing reporters graffiti tags in which the word "anti-social" had been corrected to read "antisocial."

"The deadly territory dispute between these two organizations, as well as the notorious MLA Handbook gang, has claimed the lives of more than 63 publishing professionals this year alone."

Officials also stated that an innocent 35-year-old passerby who found himself caught up in a long-winded

*dispute over use of the serial, or Oxford, comma had died
of a self-inflicted gunshot wound.*
*http://www.theonion.com/articles/4-copy-editors-killed-
in-ongoing-ap-style-chicago,30806/*

Love,
Melissa

July 31

I have this image of several withered scholars ringed by
stacks of books in an ill-lit room, dust motes in the air, pon-
dering the value and future of punctuation. It starts with the
poor em dash, and then you know where it will go next . . .
yes, the majestic semicolon.

THIS TYRANNY MUST STOP! Do what you will, but leave
the semicolon untouched. I beg you . . . whimper.

Chris

August 11

The young man waited for 10 minutes in front of the desks
of aged and molting professors, The Keepers of the Language.
        Finally, frustrated, he said, "I have literally been wait-
ing here for like 30 minutes."
        To this comment angry eyes arched over the books
in front of the professors, who spoke in unison, "Child, that
was the improper use of the word 'literally,' and if you say
'like' again we will have you forcibly removed."
        The young man responded, "Really? . . . Whatever."
        Steam rose from behind the books as the tempera-
ture in the room dropped precipitously. "GUARDS!" yelled
the professors, spewing dust and mold in the air.

The door slammed open and the young man was dragged by his feet from the room and flung from the building.

Thus ended Mack Simpson's short academic career at The University. His every waking moment was filled with thoughts of revenge as he delivered his box of goods to its destination and picked up another box for another location. A mind-numbing job that occupied the lives of millions in this land of exactitude. All boxes must be 4 feet by 4 feet and all trucks were built to accommodate one 4 foot by 4 foot box. The highways were filled with thousands of trucks running from one place to another with the exact same sized box. Why no bigger and why no smaller? No one really remembers, but when you established a standard in the Land of Exactitude there was no deviation.

Then a partially formed idea came to Mack: if he could shatter just one standard perhaps the whole system would crumble, and he would exact his revenge on the core of the Land of Exactitude and the controlling faction, The Keepers of the Language.

Mack spent hours working on his plans. He thought outside the box . . . he experimented and failed, which heretofore was unheard of. Finally, after years of work and months of bribing officials (in exact amounts), he was able to launch his new business, which used massive 18-wheeled vehicles to deliver products to his customers. Suddenly the transportation business was in turmoil, which in turn upset the box industry, and so on . . . Thousands of people were out of business, economies collapsed, mayhem ensued.

Out of this chaos a new nation was born. Where things didn't need to be exact . . . to be perfect. Things did not have to be done to perfection the first time. You could start a business with only a semi-coalesced idea; you could choose not to go to school and be semi-literate; you could start a nation by inventing the semi-trailer; and you could use the semi-colon to your heart's desire.

This excerpt from the history of our great nation was provided by The Institute of Trucking and Change, funded by Mack Truck Industries. The entire history can be found at their website, which is only partially complete.
Chris

August 12
I was pleasantly, wonderfully caught off guard as Chris' beautiful, satin dueling glove slapped across my face.
Cut to Tim walking 10 paces, gun drawn. Oh, it's on.
Tim

August 12
I believe you might have meant: "Cut to Tim; gun drawn."
Me thinks he feels the shock of my emailed fist . . . n'est-ce pas?
Chris

August 13
Deutsches Archaologisches Institut
Commission for Ancient History and Epigraphy
Amalienstrasse 73b
Munich, Germany 80799

Dear Doctor Christof Schuler,

I am an Assistant Professor of Paleography at the University of Southern North Dakota and I have long admired your published articles and lecture papers. Your ground breaking monograph on the early Sumerian use of the dash as discovered in stone tablets at Jemdet Nasr was revelatory and is now required reading for my undergraduate students.

I am writing to you to propose a collaborative effort on what I hope is an equally exciting discovery. In my recent detailed examination of the paintings at the Cave of Beasts in Gilf Kebir, Egypt I have identified what seems

to be a proto-comma and a proto-colon used both figura-
tively and epigraphically to separate man and beast.

I believe that this early use of the comma and the colon
in Paleolithic drawings and paintings is affirmation of
paleo-man's nascent understanding of language structure and developing cognizance of the need to
communicate effectively. The examination of other cave
paintings in both Northern Africa and Spain, could provide further unequivocal proof that the comma and the

colon were a unifying communicative precedent for early man.

I look forward to discussing this with you in person at the Ugartic Studies and Northwest Semitic Epigraphy Seminar in San Diego this coming November.

Sincerely Yours,
Melissa Naegelin

August 14
I checked urban legends and this pish posh appears to be a hoax propagated by Fox. In other words it may be crap.
Chris

August 14, a little later
Actually there may be something to Melissa's letter and enclosure. I sent a note to a friend at Fox and he floated the letter and enclosure around and I am surprised at the responses. They really seemed focused on the enclosure:

"I think I have found the key to the Hurricane Katrina death camps." --Beck

"Looks like an ink blot; I think I see Russia." --Palin

"This might be a map to the missing birth certificate." --Trump

"Those pictures make me feel so peaceful; they make me want to be nice." --O'Reilly

"I think those spots are animal crap." --Rivera

Who knew?

Chris

August 15

See, this is why I joined academia. To get away from petty arguments and in-fighting like this.

Love,
Assistant Professor Naegelin

September 10

Securing Our Northern Borders

AP September 10, 2014. There has been an alarming increase in the border trafficking of punctuation. Two weeks ago, a kilo of ~ was discovered in the wheel wells of an RV attempting to enter the US at the El Paso border crossing. Officials claim that this was the largest attempted shipment to date.

While much of the focus on illegal punctuation smuggling has been on the southern borders, there is also a little known but potentially more dangerous situation brewing on our northern border. Canada is now the single largest source for semi-colon smuggling into the US.

Dr. David Brickman, Professor of International Economics at Hollister Community College, states that the primary source for these semi-colons is Wales. "The Welsh economy was devastated in the EU collapse and many desperate farmers began to convert their devalued vowels into the more lucrative semi-colon."

The Welsh cartels use fishing boats to smuggle the semi-colons from Wales to Labrador and then they are re-packaged for entry into the US, according to Brian Pledgin, assistant director of US/Canadian border coordination at Homeland Security. "The amounts coming across the border are small right now, but it is only a matter of time before we start seeing larger shipments as the smugglers become more sophisticated," he added.

Amelia Sandras knows full well the destruction and sorrow that semi-colons from Canada can bring to a community. She is the director of the DeGraw Street Youth Center in Brooklyn, New York. "The kids around here were using commas and periods and sometimes co-lons. A year or so ago, we started to see semi-colon use really take a jump. "

The New York legislature has also taken notice and a bill is pending to criminalize the possession and distribution of the semi-colon. "I think we have enough votes to get this very important law passed," said Demo-cratic State Senator Donna Tranchard.

Melissa

September 10

They are on to me. I will have to find the next big thing. It appears that semi-colons may have become very run of the mill; so un-indie. When you start to see this level of punctu-ation smuggling you need to jump ship. It is only a matter of days before the NSA has compiled a complete dossier of punctuation usage and they ship you off to the hoosegow. (I have always wanted to use the word hoosegow in a sen-tence). They will tie up your finances for months looking for a misplaced period hiding as a decimal on your balance sheets. Just a matter of time. . . .

Chris

September 11

Officer Decker awoke with a slight start. Always a light sleeper – always vigilant to protect the one place, the one real "beat", he felt he could control in his life – he was prone to waking throughout any night he hadn't been drinking.

Usually he would imagine a terrible situation that would allow him to single-handedly save the family. A fire tearing through the cheap furniture in the living room; blocking the stairs with a furnace of terror. A meth-fueled gang of murderers.

His body, hyper-alert, would start to hear, smell, imagine what was never there. No whiff of smoke, after all. No light jingle of a Harley key fob from the front porch.

In reality, it was his own fart that woke him up. He was a night-farter. While we're coming clean on the subject he was a day-farter, too. As well as a dawn and dusk farter. He even owned the nooner and the midnighter; those mystery worlds of neither PM nor AM.

He was a great farter. Or a terrible farter. Depending on your appreciation of the subject. And apparently this trait just might have skipped a generation.

His grandfather was from Brooklyn. Canarsie. Which only sounds nice. As was Decker's father. And when his father referred to HIS father in a story he called him "my fahtuh". So everyone just assumed.

At the precinct a "10-27" was jokingly used when a peculiar smell was reported. 1027 being Decker's badge number.

But this was not just a fart. This was an intruder. The real deal. Go time.

In fact, he/she/it was slowly coming up the stairs to the second floor. Reaching around quickly, Decker found his night stick, silently slid to the doorway of his bedroom, and clicked on the lights for the upstairs landing.

It was Phillip. His teenage son. Who was now shocked to see his father holding a long back massager wand; held aloft and now thrumming with a low-pitched and intermittent buzz.

jesus dad are you okay you scared me

Father and son simultaneously realized that Phillip's utterance had no punctuation. Phillip retreated quickly to his bedroom but Decker's foot prevented the door from closing behind Phillip. Slowly pushing the door open, Decker turned off the vibrating wand with a click and searched his son's eyes for the truth, or deceit, or clues, or something.

dad im tired can we just talk in the morning

"My God", said Decker. "I spend every day up to my elbows in the filth of punctuation abuse. And it's right here. Under my own roof. What'd you do with it all? Tell me! Are you . . . ?"

im selling it okay are you happy you solved it big man

"You capitalized . . . all your punctuation? Sweet Jesus."

Decker noticed Phillip glance at his dresser drawers against the wall. And Phillip noticed Decker notice him. They both rushed to the top drawer. Decker overpowered the teen and pulled the drawer out as hard as he could.

A rain of little baggies filled with periods, commas and parenthesis fell to the floor. A baggie filled with exclamation points and labeled "SHOUT" fell with a heavy thud at Decker's feet.

"How much are you selling it for?" croaked Decker. There was no need to pretend anymore.

commas and periods for 5

dashes and parenthesis for 10

20 for the big guns like question marks and exclamation points

semi colon goes for 50

"What about the colon?"

for some reason nobody wants to snort a colon dad

"Well it all ends here, son."

At that, Decker picked a stray period off of Phillip's cheek and held it up on his finger tip to Phillip.

Phillip nodded. Decker smiled. He turned off the lights and padded slowly to his room in the dark. Somehow, the wand in his hand turned on again. Clicking it off, Decker slid into bed, closed his eyes and drifted into a deep sleep, even as a lone, loud fart rang out.

Thus he didn't hear the light jingle of a Harley key fob on the front porch; nor the door open; nor would he smell the faint whiff of smoke.

Tim

_____

6/5

Ah the lowly semi-colon. Once so valued, yet now I have come to realize that it pales in comparison to its stronger cousin the colon:

The colon that is so powerful and strong . . . that tells us that something momentous and official is about to be bespoke. And its true glory is that it is not only punctuation, but also a vital organ. So vital that it is often observed by our physician friends through a most remarkable feat of modern medicine: the scope. Who doesn't remember the first time, after the glorious age of 50, that we had our first colonoscopy? Again momentous and oh so official. And perhaps reported by our Mater on a Facebook post along with her toe.

All of this to say, the sad semi-colon has been pushed from its dais and now rests, shattered at the foot (or toe) of the colon. I shall sing its praises into the night as I mourn the loss of the semi-colon.

Farewell friend semi-colon; hello friend colon

Chris

Melissa Naegelin lives near Boston, where she is Senior Financial Analyst, Northeast Region, for a national power company.

Christopher Roan was a lost cause and major source of discouragement and pain to his parents until the age of 18. Then he joined the Army, loved it, and 30 years later, retired as a Colonel (Note the mighty Colon is present at the end of his career).

tim roan makes advertising in New York City. and it's the best advertising ever done. of course this is according to his mom. and that's the only praise he needs. after all, gold trophies don't give lengthy, comforting hugs. tim will die alone in Debtor's Prison.

Carol Roan never thought she raised her three children. Rather, she watched them grow up singing, fighting, telling stories, acting out bad movies, and laughing. Melissa learned to tell stories with numbers; Chris told his men stories on night maneuvers; and Tim became a storyteller by trade.

{ 7 } 1st Place Flash Fiction

Through Time, Tide, and Turmoil

by Jennifer Bean Bower

Once, while resting on the heated shore of Mauritius, I was captured by a ruthless mob and cast into a caliginous, damp pit. Soon after, a near constant motion pushed me forward, backward, and side to side. With each nauseating action, my body became bruised and broken as it struck those around me. Yes, there were others in that tomb-like cell, and most were like me. This realization came when a faint beam of light pierced the wooden wall of my enclosure and I at once beheld the others—hundreds upon hundreds of them! In utter despair, my soul cried out to God and begged for release.

On a star-crossed day, I know not when or why, all movement ceased suddenly. Without warning, an unknown force seized my body and carried it down—ever so deeply down—to the watery grave that waited. For an eternity I lay in a wet comatose state until a great surge uplifted my body and spewed it on dry ground. At last! Dry ground! Overflowing with joy, I basked in the warmth of the heavenly sun and praised it without end. Eventually, that star in all its power, abolished each damp morsel from my core.

Of course, new beginnings have their challenges and mine had many. Marooned and alone, that place—that beach—was void of others like me. Although there was an air of familiarity, my surroundings were foreign. The tan-colored sand was cluttered with debris; the landscape was barren; and the sea did not sparkle, but exhibited a greenish-blue hue. On certain days, more oft than not, countless humans—unlike any I had ever seen—surrounded me. Thanks be to God, most never noticed my presence. Occasionally; however, the smaller of the species would hoist me from the ground and carry me about in some strange conveyance. Inevitably, by day's end, I was returned to the earth.

Countless days passed when the atmosphere turned cool and the humans were seen less often. Gladness filled my heart and I began contemplating a peaceful existence on that dry shore; but, destiny did not permit it. A human, one of the large types, collected my body and began bounding towards the sea. Every cell of my being pleaded for mercy, as I knew the mouth of that aqueous hell would soon consume me once more. Arriving at the water's edge, my captor stopped—and to my great surprise did nothing—my body was neither dropped nor hurled. The creature looked back and forth between the sea and me until it at last proclaimed, "It cannot be. It just cannot be!"

With great haste, the human wrapped my body in a soft fabric and placed me inside an odd-looking machine. On course towards an unknown destination, I wondered to what abyss my body would soon be given. Within the hour, I was laid on a cold, silver table and the wrapping which covered me was undone. A circle of humans peered down, so closely down on me, I nearly choked in their breath. The creatures sang praises to the one who had brought me there and words with unknown meanings flowed from their lips; words like basalt, ballast, and volcanic. For days, I passed from one human hand to another, as my body was weighed, measured and scraped. Then, the creatures gathered 'round me once more. An older of the species lifted my body upward and announced, "This ballast stone is the most significant treasure ever found on a North Carolina beach. It proves the shipwreck we have long searched for indeed lies off our shore. The grant is ours!"

Flashes of light came and went, while the humans cheered my existence. In the spotlight of it all, I wondered what I had been part of, what history my body would tell, and how these humans would treat me. To them, at least on this day, I was an object of fascination, desire—a treasure.

For now, my body is at rest on a plush, sand-colored material within a dry, glass-like case. I pray my journey has reached its end and hope the others—those still imprisoned by the sea—shall find their way here and to me. Godspeed my friends.

{ 8 } 1ˢᵗ Place Poetry

Breast Stroke

By Janet Joyner

Portrait d'une négresse, 1800.
--- Marie-Guilhelmine Benoist

On one wall of the Musée du Louvre
among the gargantuan Jacques-Louis Davids,
the Delacroixs and Gericaults, two exquisitely
blank, signifying eyes stare out of your modest
frame and ask me to read you, seated there on that
almost concealed *ancien régime* chair, like a hieroglyph
of some exotic bird in distress, a naked black
woman in white headdress, white head-wrap
like a Phrygian cap that does say something
of helmets and courage, of brief, recently won
liberté, égalité, before Marie's paint can dry
and the little Corsican will deny with his Code
your road to identity; and a third eye, the black
nipple of your bared, black, still un-severed breast
aiming straight for the Amazon of my heart,
and I understand, I finally know,
in my white skin know, how subversion
is always the mole tunneling
between a hawk and a buzzard.

43

{ 9 } 2nd Place Poetry

A Single Page from the History of Hands

By Jennie Mejan

A burnished coat of red clay keeps her palm from breathing.
It's a hand like a statue's, carved then weathered; she holds it out for me:
twelve honey ants globed with sweetness lie drunk inside.

-

Meat is cold, mostly through with life. He cuts across its left-over resistance,
imagines missing, catching his thumb. Would the butcher's wife
recognize her true love's unextraordinary opposable in a line-up?

-

The muscle crouched between thumb and finger bone shouldn't cramp
before he's done stroking the bowing woman's robe with sapphire blue.
The painter keeps his brush pincer-tight over the urn's raw frieze.

-

Pressed together in a private way, a row upon another row of hands
rest in the laps of saffron robes. Quiet, along with blood circling fingertips
and palms feeding pulses to each other, invites transcendence.

-

She didn't notice adversity sucking slowly at the vigor of her hands.
Contrasted against the warm, busy hands of her neighbor, her own felt empty.
Her neighbor had picked one up, tried wrapping reassurance around its fingers.

-

A father's pointer finger cracks his son's personal space repeatedly. It is a
cymbal,
vibrating against peace; a voiceless member that tells the boy everything he
believes
his father wants to make clear. He hates the man, the ring, and the appendage.

-

The meaty heart of both hands sting, slapped against the stretched hide of a
goat.
The contact wakes his soul to a percolating *huh ha huh u hu*, a throb
channeled from the air to drum to core through his instrument-hands.

-

{ 10 }3rd Place Poetry

Unquilting Be

By Deborah Johnson Wood

A blanket of colorful cotton squares
spreads outward across my sewing table.
Pastel meadow well past its bloom.
Bunched-up hills, threadbare valleys,
row-upon-row of frazzled greens,
sun-bleached yellows,
dusty pinks as thin
as a spring sky.

My mother-in-law's quilt,
each separate square arranged
artfully by hue across her bed.
Then arranged again.
And again --
while the point of her tongue
held her upper lip in place --
until finally,
she connected them with
hours of white stitches
sewn eight to an inch.

"The Amish get eleven," she'd told me,
a ring of awe in her voice.
"I always think I'll get

47

at least nine."

For thirty years, we've made love
under its warmth,
tucked-up fevered children on the sofa,
giggled and wept through movies
wrapped in its smooth folds,
transformed our living room floor --
now a game table for six,
now a picnic party,
now a rainy-day nest
complete with picture book,
dog, and cat.

But today,
I survey a minefield
dotted with holes and
tattered flags.
Beside me,
a fresh stack of cotton squares,
a bit of batting.

With my best embroidery scissors
in trembling hand,
and my upper lip held
tight by the point of my tongue,
I bend,
snip one stitch,
then two,
counting as I go,
all the way to eight.
Then to eight again.
Releasing fabrics fragile as old love letters
inch
by inch.

{ 11 } Honorable Mention Poetry

Elizabethan Sonnet: Heron/Hope

By DD Upchurch

I watched a grey-blue heron graze the sky

And thought: He does not brood about the air,

Or fret if ready wings have pow'r to fly,

Or curse elusive fish, 'til worn by care,

He wearies of his wading haunts in reeds,

Where round him in the water low clouds lie.

No! His reflection shows him all he needs:

His nimble legs, sharp beak, instinctive eye.

Then I, who'd flown not far, nor crashed to earth,

But grounded airy verse with leaden fears,

Who'd stilled my budding words upon their birth,

And mourned the waste of seven wordless years,

    Hurling my dread and doubts upon the wind,

    Unfurled a fledgling hope to fly again.

{ 12 } Honorable Mention Poetry

Young Cezanne Hears too Much, Conceives "The Black Clock"

By Jennie Mejan

"Wife, that boy's brush can't conjure warmth,
like a fur hat, a solid post in a court of law,
or something he can eat."
　　"Be careful, dear husband, your son will paint you
　　trapped inside a mountain, its corridors all black-
　　ened,
　　and then he'll leave."

His father, he sketched out
first, making his head a ticking clock
small and wound to mark and yellow
the minutes that marched them to his tomb.
He painted him a case, solid like a pine box,
tucked all his blackness in the corner.

He'd always seen his mother
with her insides opened out, like a conch
showing a peachy tenderness too ripe to touch
for fear it would cave in—that's how he perched her,
delicate and hard on restful whites, needs in reach.

{ 13 } Honorable Mention Poetry

Entreaty to Young Editors

By Alice Osborn

Remember, folks, the delete key is your whacker
against acyrologia. You've killed a roach before, right?
Same thing.

Mr. Fornaciari, my sixth grade English teacher,
grew up poor in Boston and watched *I Love Lucy* re-runs
every day after school. When roaches crawled over his legs
he smooshed them with a tennis racket.
He said they smelled like apples gone bad.

Back in college and high on pot,
I flung a giant roach off my balcony
by making a toe claw with my right foot.

Years later while hosting an open mic
in downtown Raleigh,
Some in our audience jumped
like marionettes caught in turbulence.
Before the fat sucker could slink into a wall crack,
I killed him with the sign-up clipboard.

Compadres, to be a great editor,
lay waist all over the keyboard,
in your intimate and fare wisdom,
ring your fingers as the fumes
waif their decent and whale
like Lucy gobbling palates
of chocolate roaches
too sweet for her pallet.

{ 14 } 1st Place Non-Fiction

Altered Mental Status

by Keith Menhinick

I grew up in a smattering of Southern Baptist churches, and I still hear those proselytizing voices in my head, telling me to have more faith and pray harder. Well, I'm not sure who lied—God or them—but something did not line up. For months, I prayed for God to heal my mother. God, please. I prayed it as often as I breathed. As Mama's sickness worsened, prayer became more and more arduous, my awareness of God more and more obscure. I doubted the point of my prayers, and the act of quieting my mind and kneeling down in supplication before a mute God felt increasingly more delusional.

My every intellectual sensibility resisted prayer as if it belonged in the same category as tarot cards and crystal balls. Doesn't psychology explain it all as a pacifying construct to control emotions and thoughts? The value of prayer seemed to lie in its connection to meditation, the practice of stilling one's mind and opening one's inner eye to greater self- and other-awareness. The mind is as difficult to control as the wind—the Bhagavad Gita says—and yet our task is to try, because it is the only thing we have any control of at all.

Meditation? Sure. But prayer? Prayer was reserved for the white-washed, think-dependent evangelicals of my childhood, the same ones who hated the gays, the immigrants, and the feminists. Prayer was reserved for those who viewed God as an omnipotent puppeteer in unquestioned control of human life, for those who said things like "everything happens for a reason." I simply did not believe in that God anymore. That God was nowhere near my Mama in the hospital these past few months, and I was calling bullshit on the whole "keep faith" and "pray harder" idea.

But maybe the real difficulty in prayer was never intellectual. The more I saw Mama's body deteriorate and her spirit crumble, the more I felt a deep anger boil in my stomach. I spent years serving in the Church, and now here I was in my first-year of graduate studies at Wake Forest Divinity; here I was giving my life to preparing for full-time ministry and vocational service to God. And where was God! Mama had no reason to be sick. She was a nurse with habits of exercise and clean eating. Any day, Mama should have improved, the doctors should have found answers, the medicines should have started working. The more I saw Mama suffer, the more my anger grew at the God who was supposed to be able to heal her.

And yet, whenever I found myself at the edge of my ability to make sense of life, whenever fear formed knots in my stomach and turned the bones in my knees to Jell-O, I found myself on the floor with the suspicious but familiar words of prayer on my tongue. Seeing Mama in pain riled anger in me and it put me on my knees. As though guided by invisible strings, or maybe by childlike routine, the muscles of my angry body and brain fell into their rehearsed places, and I found myself praying to a God I was not sure was present to listen. God, heal my mother, and if you cannot, bring her relief. Please.

That's the state I was in when my father called me: "I'm so sorry to tell you this, but they're rushing your mom to a hospital in Chapel Hill. They've done all they can here in Charlotte, and you know she hasn't gotten any better. This morning the nurse tried to wake her up to check her vitals and…" Dad paused. Then continued, "Well she was supposed to have another spinal tap this morning. The meningitis takes so much out of her, and she finds no relief from the pounding in her head. We're used to her trying to sleep it off, but this morning the nurse could barely wake her up. By the time she was up, she could only open one eye and couldn't speak. She just kind of moaned. We knew something was wrong, that it wasn't just the meningitis."

Dad's voice was uncharacteristically tentative. "Dad, please tell me," I cajoled him. He sighed into the phone.

"Looks like she had a dozen mini-strokes. Something about the inflammation from the meningitis blocking blood flow to her brain. They're rushing her to Memorial Hospital in Chapel Hill and assembling a team of doctors from UNC and Duke. Your aunt and I did our best to follow the ambulance in our cars, but it was flying. We're both here now though, and Grandmother is on the way."

Dad convinced me to finish out my final classes for the day before hopping into the car and driving to Chapel Hill. The whole drive I prayed for Mama, but the more I prayed, the more my prayers shortened. I struggled to find the right, most sincere words. I could think of only two: God, please. A desperate mantra and endless soundtrack of my panicked and reckless speeding. An hour and a half later, I arrived at the hospital. Dad met me in the lobby, and I did my best to smile.

"Hey, my son." He kissed my temple and filled me in on the way up to the seventh floor. "There's something you need to know before you go in. The strokes caused…well, it caused some memory loss, mostly short-term memory. She hasn't been able to recognize anyone since they got her stabilized. And she keeps hallucinating."

He hesitated. "You don't have to come in and see her. She is still really nauseous too—keeps throwing up. We can get a hotel room tonight, and maybe she will be better tomorrow."

"Dad, I'm 24. You don't have to protect me like you do my little brothers. I'm fine," I spouted back to him, a little too quickly and a little too irritated.

"Okay. This is hard for me, hard to know what to do. Tell me if this is too much, if you want to know less."

"Never. I want to know everything. Really, I'm okay," I said, and I spent the rest of the few minutes up to Mama's room trying to convince myself of it.

We reached the Critical Care Unit and walked past the nurse's station to the last unit on the small hallway—no. 4. The walls of the unit were all glass, and I could see Mama sitting up in the bed. Mama's sister sat in the cream leather armchair on the opposite side of the bed. Her mother sat in a chair against the window, applying a fresh coat of lipstick with a pocket mirror.

Dad and I paused at the door. My eyes latched onto three words written on pink paper and taped to the glass door beneath the "No. 4" sign. The three words were written in all caps, which felt like someone screaming at me: "ALTERED MENTAL STATUS." The words were so medical, yet they gripped me in the throat. I felt like I couldn't breathe. Whatever resolve I had worked up was immediately shaken. Those three words became pictures in my head; pictures that made my imagination run wild with recycled images from old movies. I imagined asylums with lunatics locked in trying to eat their own toes and burn down houses to kill invisible mice and...

"You okay?" Dad asked, resting his hand on my shoulder.

"Yeah, I'm cool. Can we go in?" I was determined to be strong.

We were barely two steps into the room, when my mother cried out, "Ah! Did you come from the walls!?" Her eyes bulged and she pulled her neck back behind her shoulders like she was trying to decide if we were either the nastiest things she had ever seen or the meanest.

She quickly dropped her eyes from us to the picc lines slithering out of her arms. "What the heck! What are these?" Mama squeezed her forehead and wrinkled her nose with disgust, then began to move her left hand towards her right arm's picc line. Aunt Kathryn grabbed her hand firmly, but gently.

"No, baby girl. These are here to make you better. You have to leave them in."

"Really?" Mama asked, and her face wore a childlike look of genuine confusion.

"Really, really," Aunt Kathryn said. She left her hand resting on top of Mama's, then looked up at me, smiling. "She's been doing this all day. Hey kiddo."

I hugged my aunt and grandmother, then knelt down beside the bed.

"Hey Mama. How are you feeling?"

"Why is this nurse calling me his Mama? I'm like…the same age as him!" Mama said it like she was a comedian on stage, looking around the room, person to person, and fishing for a laugh. Suddenly, she saw Dad standing behind me. "Whoa! Is that Barry White?!"

I wasn't sure yet if I was allowed to laugh, and I wasn't sure if I even wanted to, but Aunt Kathryn sure did. My dad is white and tone-deaf. I gave a half-smile and made room for him next to the hospital bed.

"No, silly," Dad chuckled. "It's me, your handsome husband!" He kissed her on the forehead.

"Ha!" Mama started giggling, presumably due to Barry White's kiss. She then put her hand on the side of her face like she was telling a secret, though she did not even try to whisper. "I think my husband's gay."

Aunt Kathryn howled at this. We all did. It was so different from the usual scene of Mama moaning and crying in pain, so unexpected now to see her laughing and cracking jokes, even if they weren't exactly jokes to her.

"Com'ere, Barry White! Sing your smooth tunes to me! Well, don't sing too much, because it'll make me wanna' have sex."

"Mama!" I cried out, horrified.

"Tricia!" Grandmother gasped with, I imagine, the same horrified look I was wearing. Grandmother stood up, showing to the room her offense that such an indecent comment could come from a daughter of hers. Dad loved it. He grinned from ear to ear, leaned in, and drenched himself in it.

"I'm going to step out for a few," I offered, "let y'all handle whatever it is that's happening right now." And with that, I stepped out of the room, following Grandmother who had gathered her things and made her exit.

That night, Aunt Kathryn refused to leave Mama's side, so the rest of us stayed in the hotel around the corner. Dad and I shared a room, and he went straight to sleep. I lay silent under the blankets, trying to pray and tossing around in my head those three words from the pink paper on Mama's door. The more I thought about it, the angrier I got. Not only was her body fighting against itself, but now her mind was slipping too? Where are you God! The voice in my head screamed and hurled more questions at the silent God. I brewed in my anger all night long, as if that would force God's hand.

The next morning, Dad and Grandmother went up to Mama's room so I could "make some phone calls in the lobby." Instead, I walked to the corner stall of the fourth floor bathroom.

I planted the toe of my shoe on the silver handle and flushed, letting the noise of the toilet drown out my sighs. I flushed again, and pent-up tears spilled down my cheeks. I could not let them see me cry. I flushed again. I could not let them hear the sobs choking out from my throat. I flushed again. This was my safe haven—this fourth floor bathroom stall. I flushed again. Here, alone, I could be weak. I could be surrounded by the constant reverberation of the gargling water spinning, spinning, spinning, and disappearing. I flushed again.

God, I started to pray. I found only emptiness. I tried to repeat my "God, please" mantra, but my thoughts kept getting jumbled up. It felt like I was looking for a coin at the bottom of a creek while someone muddied it up with a giant stick. I couldn't pray, and I didn't want to. I flushed again. A wave of guilt gushed in, and I felt like a great phony. Here I was in Divinity School, studying religion, preparing to be a minister, and I couldn't perform the faith's most elementary practice. What a poser. I needed a warning sign over the glass door of my life, cautioning people to steer the hell away, or at least a sign reading: "ALTERED SPIRITUAL STATUS." I flushed again. My belief in God was treacherously low, and instead I felt more hot anger swell in my chest. I could not see God anywhere in this. I flushed again. Fifteen minutes, then get it together, I told myself.

I climbed the stairs to the seventh floor, and Dad and Aunt Kathryn were waiting for me in the hallway. Dad said, "Mom is still disoriented, but, thank God, she's laughing. Her team of doctors came in early this morning. White blood cells still off. Spinal tap later." Dad sighed deeply, then continued, "I'm stepping out with Kathryn to grab some breakfast. Apparently she was up all night." Dad looked at Aunt Kathryn.

"Yeah, Tricia kept thinking she was steering a runaway car," Aunt Kathryn said as she motioned with her hands. "She sat up in the bed all night, pressed her feet against the foot bar of the bed like it was a break pedal, and she flipped the steering-wheel pillow over and over. She was literally screaming at the top of her lungs, pulling and pressing and steering and thinking she was about to wreck. I am exhausted."

"Oh wow," I said. "Well, get some food and rest."

"I'll try. Call me if one of the doctors comes back. We still haven't talked to the infectious disease doctor. We'll be back before she has the spinal tap."

"Sounds good. I'll hold down the fort here." And with that, they disappeared down the hall.

Mama and I met eyes as I looked through the glass walls. She was sitting upright in the hospital bed, which had been raised at the head, and Grandmother was perched in the chair beside her. My eyes hit the pink sign on the glass wall again: "ALTERED MENTAL STATUS." Three deep breaths, three pumps of hand sanitizer, and I slid the glass door to the side, stepped into No. 4, rested my backpack against the wall, and whispered, "Hey Mama."

Mama's eyes widened: "Woooow, you look just like my son!"

My heart skipped a little. Maybe her memory was coming back. I leapt at the hope that her mind was returning, "I am your son, Mama! It's me!"

Mama reached up and touched my cheek with her hand. Her fingers on my face felt like bones—cold and brittle—and they moved with curiosity. Her forehead scrunched as she tried to think. I sensed that the simple movement dispensed disproportionate energy from her depleted reserves. The moment over, she looked away and her hand fell back to her lap. Mama chuckled softly and shook her head, speaking aloud though seemingly to herself. "Boy, you sure do look like him. I swear you nurses just get younger and younger."

Grandmother stood up. "Oh Tricia, you know that's your son."

Mama side-eyed Grandmother in response. "And you would know? Sheesh, doctors think they know everything these days." Mama laughed to herself and leaned back against her pillows. Grandmother stared at me with a serious look of both concern and shock, as if no one had ever spoken to her this way before. I shrugged and sat down.

Later that day, as more and more family arrived at the hospital, I began to realize that my mother was sicker than Dad was letting on. Normally he turned visitors away.

All day we leaned on walls, rested in chairs, sat on the floor, and surrounded Mama's hospital bed while she slept. Aunt Kathryn rested her eyes in the leather recliner. The rest of us held space, and none of us said a word. I sat against the wall, staring at my shoes and making eye contact with no one. I was so scared—scared Mama would never recognize me again; scared we would lose her forever. I barely contained the urge to cry.

Then, softly, just above a whisper, Grandmother started to sing:

"O Lord, my God, when I in awesome wonder

Consider all the worlds Thy hands have made."

Mama woke up. Her eyelids slid open. The sound of singing sparked something in her, and she sat up in the hospital bed. She began to nod her head back and forth and snap her fingers like she was listening to jazz. The rest of the family began to sing softly with Grandmother, and I saw Dad, mouthing the words with his eyes closed.

"I see the stars, I hear the rolling thunder,

Thy power throughout the universe displayed."

My family sang on at a slow, somber tempo, but Mama danced like she was in a swing club. She bounced her head, snapped her fingers, swayed her shoulders, her energy increasing with every snap. Soon her dancing started to mix with laughter. Then my family hit the chorus, and their notes and volume rose.

"Then sings my soul, my Savior God, to Thee,

How great Thou art, How great Thou art."

At this point in the song, Mama was really feeling it! Her bouncing and snapping and swaying crescendoed with each added voice in the room. By the time they hit the chorus, Mama was doing body rolls. That's right—my sick mother, confined to a hospital bed, totally out of her mind, started doing body rolls to How Great Thou Art. Grandmother must have thought it all a scandal. Catheter and IV lines flung precariously, and Mama body rolled.

"Then sings my soul, my Savior God, to Thee,

How great Thou art, How great Thou art."

And Mama was still body rolling. By now, her own dancing had cracked her up, and she laughed hysterically like she was ten. We all started smiling at Mama, at the sheer absurdity of her dancing and laughing. Then, from somewhere deep inside us, erupted a laughter that caught us all. Even Grandmother giggled a little. We laughed, body rolled, and sang hymns.

Suddenly, Mama stopped dancing. "The nurses here are so weird," she said, shaking her head. "Thank you, but please stop so I can sleep." With that, Mama rested her face against the pillow, fell asleep, and the room fell silent.

Just then, one of Mama's nurses came into the room. She reached up the IV pole to lift one of the solution bags off of its hook. She eyed the little bit of fluid left in the bag and began to switch it out with a new one. While she worked, she spoke quietly to the room.

"You know, I work with a lot of patients with 'Altered Mental Status.' Whatever bad you got inside of you, I swear it brings it out. People lose control of their mental faculties and they start saying whatever comes to mind. Some people get plain mean, saying the most hurtful things they ever thought of their family members." The nurse hooked a new bag to the IV pole. "But all Tricia does is laugh! Y'all are lucky."

She finished her work and left the room, and I continued to sit against the wall. Spending all that time with Mama in the hospital, seeing her body and mind slowly mutiny, changed me. I felt so distant from God—so angry at a God so absent. But for a moment, when Grandmother started singing, and Mama started dancing, God finally showed up. Or maybe God had been there all along and my slow eyes had finally caught up. I felt it in the pit of my stomach, the way you feel when you walk the stage at graduation or finish the last coat of paint on a new apartment. Assurance. For the first time since I arrived at NC Memorial Hospital, I noticed how all the tears and pain of sickness had been relieved with laughter. There was so much laughter in that room! So much family, so much love!

It was a moment of perfect peace. Maybe that is all we get in this complicated world. Moments. Never here to stay, never promised to return. It was a moment I tried to cling to, to hold against my bones, but there it went, slipping into sleep with Mama. It may have only lasted a moment, but it was real. For that one moment, I believed in God again.

{ 15 } 2nd Place Non Fiction

Shock Treatment and the Reluctant Traveler

By Mark Mathosian

In the 1960's some psychiatric patients received electroshock therapy to help them cope. During treatment electrodes were taped to their foreheads and they were bombarded with intense jolts of electric current. I remember the first time I assisted a doctor and nurses administering shock treatment to a patient.

I was eighteen years old and employed as a psychiatric aide on an adolescent ward at Kings Park State Hospital. Most patients in the hospital were from New York City, Brooklyn and the Bronx. Transporting them to the suburbs of Long Island was considered a good idea; far enough away from their homes and friends to allow psychiatric therapy to work.

The patient scheduled for shock therapy on this particular day was housed upstairs on the third floor of my building. He was not from my ward and I was surprised to hear my name called over the intercom to escort him to another building for treatment.

After arriving at his ward the duty nurse told me that I was the only male psychiatric aide in the building. They were afraid the patient would not willingly go for shock treatment.

I walked into the dayroom and the patient was pointed out to me. I immediately recognized him from previous encounters in our building's dining room. I considered him a docile person, not prone to violence or a negative disposition.

His name was John and he was about seventeen years old. John grew up in a tough area of Brooklyn and came from a broken home in which he was often the subject of childhood beatings from an alcoholic father. At some point he was diagnosed as suffering from depression and schizophrenia and in need of institutionalized treatment. He was court committed to the Kings Park State Hospital for treatment.

Wearing state-issued clothing, John stood with his back against a wall in what looked like a catatonic state. He was over six feet tall and towered over other patients. He stood perfectly still, his glassy brown eyes focused straight ahead. His muscular arms lay motionless by his sides. I noticed that he had a cold sore on his top lip. It had scabbed over and his lips looked dry.

Catatonic schizophrenics often stand in the same spot for hours, showing little concern for their surroundings. John tuned out all of the other patients in the room. He stood motionless, as stiff as a board, in the hospital dayroom. When we reached John, the nurse introduced us.

"John, the nurse said calmly, Mr. Mathosian is here to escort you for your shock treatment."

He did not respond, nor did he turn his head to acknowledge our presence. Instead, he continued to stare straight ahead.

"What now?" I thought to myself as I turned to the nurse for guidance. She recognized the expression on my face and simply shrugged her shoulders.

"Come on John," I said firmly, and tugged on his arm. He didn't look at me and he still didn't move.

"Look, John," I said softly, "you know we have to go, so please don't give me a hard time. If you do, I am going to get help and we will put you in a strait jacket. You can come voluntarily or by force. Either way, you are going for shock treatment."

He slowly turned his head in my direction and stared down into my eyes. I stared back. Before he could respond I tugged on his shirt sleeve and started him in the direction of the ward's door. Close to his side, with his elbow in my hand, he slowly shuffled across the tiled floor. Patients in the dayroom parted the way as we inched forward.

The treatment room for shock therapy was in a building just behind ours, across a parking lot and a grassy field. The thought entered my mind that John might struggle once we were outside where I couldn't get help. Luckily, that didn't happen.

Once we were outside John peacefully walked towards our destination. As we walked along, I thought about what I had learned in training about schizophrenics and shock therapy.

Schizophrenia is one of the most common forms of psychoses. The symptoms of this mental illness include delusions, hallucinations, disorientation in vision, and thought disorder.

Schizophrenics often demonstrate irrational behavior and their delusions are typically absurd and bizarre. It is not uncommon for a patient to feel persecuted and believe someone is out to get them. Many sufferers also have delusions that they are a famous person from the past, like Napoleon or Lincoln, or that their thoughts are controlled by machines. Surprisingly, it is estimated that one to two percent of the population in a western society may sooner or later be treated for schizophrenia.

While drug therapy has been a standard method of treatment for the symptoms of this mental disorder, electroconvulsive therapy, aka shock therapy, was introduced as a stimuli for the mentally ill by two prominent Italian psychiatrists in 1937.

In its original form the treatment involved the attachment of electrodes to opposite sides of a patient's forehead and firing up a "shock machine" which sent alternating currents of electricity through the patient's head. These bolts of current, 50 to 60 cycles per second, entered the patient's brain and rendered him unconscious. Unconsciousness was followed by violent body seizures.

In more than 80% of the cases this shock treatment would cause the reality warping symptoms of schizophrenia to go away, at least temporarily. While the treatment itself has been modified over the years, the basic premise for its use remains the same. To temporarily relieve depression, delusions, and feelings of persecution. To bring sufferers back to reality, to the real world.

When John and I arrived at the other building I reached in my pocket for my large silver pass key. He stood motionless as I twisted the key in the lock and opened the metal door. John peered inside and his eyes grew large. I assumed he was remembering his last visit for shock therapy.

Soon we were greeted by two middle aged nurses dressed in white uniforms from head to toe. They introduced themselves and led us into a room where a doctor, also wearing white, was waiting. One of the nurses struck up a conversation.

"Have you ever assisted in a shock treatment session before?" she asked.

"No." I replied.

"It will be easy," she said. " All you have to do is hold down the patient's legs."

I glanced at John, who was standing next to me, but he didn't look back. Still, I believe he sensed I didn't like this any more than he did. The silence of the moment was shattered when a nurse took John's arm and motioned him to move.

Both nurses accompanied John to an adjoining room and closed the door behind them. They returned in about five minutes. Instead of wearing clothing, John now wore a hospital gown tied in the back. His socks and shoes were removed and he was led towards a white sheeted hospital bed in the middle of the room. They asked him to lie down but he wouldn't.

Instead, John stiffened and refused to move. The nurses, one on each side of him, applied pressure, but to no avail. Both turned to me.

"Great," I thought, "here we go again." I moved closer to John and whispered in his ear.

"Come on, you know we have to do this. Let's get it over with. Then, we can both get out of here."

Surprisingly, the encouragement worked. John eased himself onto the edge of the bed and slowly laid down.

The nurses motioned for me to stand at the foot of the bed near John's feet. Then we waited while the doctor gathered equipment for the treatment.

One of the nurses briefly left the room, and when she returned she was pushing a shiny aluminum cart with a metal machine sitting on top of it. The machine looked like an aluminum radio with small plastic control knobs. The contraption was, of course, the shock machine.

The shock machine was quietly rolled to a spot just behind John's head, out of his view. I watched John's eyes for any signs of recognition. There were none.

The doctor, who was now almost ready to begin, dominated the room. He quickly came to John's side and began giving directions.

"Nurse, please place the rubber mouthpiece in the patient's mouth and prepare his forehead."

Both nurses responded methodically. One wiped John's forehead with a damp cloth as the other stuffed a large rubber mouth-piece into his mouth. Once the mouthpiece was in place John began breathing loudly through his nose. Electrodes, connected by wire to the shock machine, were then taped to each side of John's forehead.

The three of us stood quietly around John and waited for the doctor's orders.

"Time to commence," he said quietly.

With a turn of the knob electrical bolts were fired into John's brain. It only took seconds, very quiet seconds. Then John started to convulse.

His entire body became as rigid as a two by four, and he rocked violently up and down on the hospital bed as his head vibrated uncontrollably on the soft cushion of the hospital mattress. His feet, which I held down at the other end of the bed, did the same thing.

I glanced at John's face. He was expressionless. He was breathing hard and mucus was blowing in and out of his nose. He was drooling slightly from the sides of his mouth. Then I noticed the blood.

"What is going on here?" I thought to myself. I looked more closely at John's face and realized what had happened.

Somehow, probably from all of the violent movements, the cold sore on John's lip had rubbed raw. It was now dripping blood and the blood was running over his bottom lip and mixing with saliva that involuntarily spurted from his mouth.

One of the nurses noticed what happened and immediately began to pat the area with a white cloth.

Then, much to my dismay, it was shock time again. The knob was twisted and POW, another surge of electricity was blasted into John's brain. As the current passed through him he once again went into convulsions and bounced uncontrollably.

This treatment was repeated one more time. John remained passive throughout the different phases, oblivious to what was going on around him, and to him. I, on the other hand, was sweating profusely. My white shirt was wet and clung to my body.

When we were finally done the nurses and I helped John sit up and they escorted him to the other room to get dressed. When they returned he was ready to be escorted back to his ward. Staring at him, I was having a difficult time comprehending what he had just been through.

As we walked down the hospital corridor towards the large entrance door I noticed a strange thing. John was walking faster, practically leading the way. Then he turned in my direction and spoke.

"Boy am I glad that's over. Let's get back to our building, I'm hungry."

I looked into John's alert eyes and smiling face. He continued talking non-stop. He jabbered about this and that as dozens of topics rolled off his tongue. I listened attentively to his words and walked in silence by his side as we made our way back to our building and his ward.

{ 16 } 3rd Place Non Fiction

Felix and the Silver Surfer

by Gary Bolick

I first met Felix twenty years ago at Roland Bennett's Lunch, across from the courthouse, on Second Street. He was angry. He had tried to pay for his white-bean soup and meatloaf sandwich with pennies. The cashier had made it a point to raise her voice, and smirk when she refused the seven faded, red, greasy, paper rolls. One slipped from his grasp, and the tiny, copper cylinders scattered like a spooked flock of geese. The noise and confusion was not unlike the honking and hissing usually associated with frightened and angry waterfowl.

I walked to the front of the line, and asked Felix if I could exchange paper money for the coins, as I was a coin collector. He frowned, wanting to escalate the argument over the refused coins, but deferred to his hunger, thanked me, spat to the side of the cashier, took his lunch, and ate it on the courthouse steps.

I watched him while I ate my own lunch. Our eyes met once, he nodded, raised his sandwich as a sort of half salute and thank-you gesture, then raised one cheek of his buttocks and farted. A beautiful young paralegal and her boss, startled by the flatulence, moved quickly to one side, but not before the lawyer, stopped, retraced his steps and confronted Felix. Leaning over him, holding his briefcase out to make his point, the moment seemed ripe for another collapse of civility, another clash between the classes, but Felix smiled. Simply remained stoic, and smiled. He continued to smile until the lawyer, fatigued and sweating, turned abruptly, and left. The exquisite paralegal rubbed his shoulders and touched his cheek to soothe him. Felix watched them for a moment, finished his beans, and laughed.

Off and on for the next several years, I watched as Felix haunted downtown. One day he would be sitting on the old bronze and oak bench in front of the Robert E. Lee Memorial situated in the town square reading Spinoza or a People Magazine. Another day his face would hover in the sun's reflection in a third story window of the firehouse or the front door of the library. Some days he would climb up on a wooden crate, one in a long line of street preachers down on the Trade Street Mall. It was a popular place in the spring to eat lunch and listen to the seven to ten different ways the world was about to end. Felix, of course, running contrary to the moment, refused to talk. He mimed his sermon. Marcel Marceau in worn khakis, a denim shirt, three days of facial hair, and a smile that can only be described as frightening. His grin had the effect of making the observer feel as though he were a foreigner, of being randomly placed in a country, or time, or inside a population that was completely alien. What did Felix see that I didn't? And how could he be so sure? And what was it, exactly, that he was so sure about?

My encounter with Felix in Roland Bennett's Lunch was to be our first and last actual meeting. During the next twenty years, we never exchanged more than eight or ten words except to say, "Nice day" or "Still hanging in there." I thought it was presumptuous of me to think that he might benefit from my acquaintance. The real reason, as I see it today, that I avoided him was that I was afraid to step out, in any meaningful fashion, from my routine. So I watched him from the lunch booth, or stopped to look for his face, or body to appear, then simply returned to my day.

Now, closing in on sixty, getting on with my day , has been not at all unpleasant; what with the children grown, and the bills no longer a chore, and the wife percolating quietly beside me as we choose how to slip into retirement, and then out of life; the effort is soft and agreeable, the challenges familiar. I guess I am like the sleeping dog off in the corner, or lying in the sun, a mutt, a conglomeration of blood and experience too lazy–now–to dream. Nothing is new or exciting–now. Everything is within a specific place and time, and that's fine. Fine until Felix bumped into me, again.

Yesterday I had to be at work early. Walking across the square, I saw someone sleeping on the Lee bench. It was too early for the sun to be completely up, but too late for the streetlights to remain illuminated. I would not have even noticed him, except for the dog. A mongrel was nervously approaching, and then retreating from the person asleep on the bench, whimpering, and then barking as he continued his anxious dance. Finally the dog latched onto the pants leg of the homeless man, and pulled. Nothing.

Walking over, I chased the dog away, and looked down and there was Felix–dead.

Huddled up, his arms wrapped around his body, his legs slightly crossed, Felix apparently had died in his sleep a few hours earlier. A spiral bound notebook with a ballpoint pen lodged inside was on the bench with him. It bothered me that I did not feel more loss at that moment, that all I could think about was that I would have to stay late after coming in early. Felix covered that, too.

Fred let me keep the notebook. Fred, the assistant to the Medical Examiner, and I had gone to school together. When I found Felix, I called him, and he arranged for the Coroner's office to pick up the body and take it down to the city morgue. When I told him that I had kept it in case Felix had some next of kin, Fred laughed, and said that if I had not called him, and given him the name Felix, the man on the bench would simply have become another John Doe before being cremated. "Keep it," he told me, "you, it appears you are the only friend he has . . . I mean, had."

After Beth went to bed, I poured myself another scotch and pulled Felix's notebook from my briefcase. Nothing has been the same since.

Every seventeen to say twenty years another Jesus, Gandhi, Buddha or Muhammad is born. Whether he-she-or-it springs to life full-grown, say maybe out of some fissure from inside of a cliff, sprung loose by an earthquake, washes up into a group of drunk fishermen on the Missouri or Yadkin rivers, comes screaming out of a tenement in Bangkok, or quietly slides out into the arms of its mother ten miles east of Birmingham A-L-A; the event, the "coming" occurs with a kind of monotonous regularity. How?

Sunspots. Part of the confounding make-up of light is that on Wednesday it is a wave while on Thursday it is a particle. The wave-particle duality isn't some riff gone awry, but a clue, a simple suggestion to look the other way when the obvious seems to be working just fine, but things, well, wait, you know things aren't as they are supposed to be . . . like Doc I feel good . . . Yeah boy, but you look bad! Um, so I guess that makes you, well, you remember the punch line. Get the picture?

Just a matter of walking it back up to the source, trace the beam up and into and around and sit, yes, sit down in the middle of that fisted mass of energy. I know, I know, like Monk said, "Trying to write about music is like dancing about architecture."

Sun spits out a particle, places it on a long wave, and the Silver Surfer rides the curl, hugs the pipeline all the way into us-here-where-some-where-any-where-usually-out-away-some-where-it-sticks. There!

Fact is, we really don't try, could care less than a rat about his, you-know-what, about recognizing or saving the right-eous-reformer-prophet, no sir! But why is that?

Too much to slice and dice, roast, broil, sauté and spice to feed the worst

in—us (all of us)—lunch. Why do you think the J-man did it over supper?

"Jesus, Mohammad, Buddha and all the rest of that pack were no different than the Motown/Stax explosion, remember? '59 to '73! In the wink of a universe looking back to scratch an itch, the odd celebrated saint or two collects easily in the wire mesh, while the others spiral down into the drain, and are ultimately whisked away and funneled down into the sewer. Confused? It's just that those particular few fit the need of the opposing wave. But original? Special? No way. How can we even begin to decide otherwise if we have already chosen this particular, opposing path? There! Another one, see?

That's the catch. It's always been one riff leads to another, the flux sets its own rhythm, place and time touching the synchronicity of its movement relative to its message. Jesus was not the first, nor the last. Remember Marvin Gaye? He was cut down, too, and by his own father, so you see it? I mean, where in the hell did his old man get that idea . . .? Maybe that's what Thomas meant when he described his holy man as being larger than the simplistic expression of self . . . jumped the arc, rode the wave clear through the Alpha and Omega and back . . . still . . . your own son? The man was right . . . who can you trust? Look past the written god where the light hooks up through one dream and time and place making them connect to one another. Curved space and the wind bringing us all back to a single point.

Ever since we stood up in those caves and started to paint, tried to fill and form the purpose of an empty imagination, we have pushed to stop, yes stop the free flowing music that was to return us back into the multi-layered fold of her womb and breast, the sweet, star-lit blanket of perfect composure, a unified message of-one-in the universe.

"The continuum is and has and will always be the rule irrespective to all–us. And what about that talking monkey, erect, and pointing at the sun? We choose a place in the shade away from the sun, now, fleeing the sliding scale of the elegant surfer. Comfortable in our wrinkle free cotton, the light-and-particle wave is treated with disgust so we miss that wondrous challenging idea or perfectly original thought presented us each day. We become the pig-in-the-pond on the brightest, hottest day-in-the-sun. Sleep, please, just let me sleep . . . well, maybe one more biscuit if you please.

Burn a rainforest to sew a crop of corn or cotton. Destroy an entangled maze of elixir and antibiotics, alchemical dreams twisting in the trees, slithering through the brush forever– lost. Jabir, the ancient Iranian wizard, weeps over the ashes, the philosophers' stone–lost. Looking up and over the horizon, he sees another surfer sliding earthward positing a space and place and time that the pig-in-the-pond ignores for the aromatic bucket of feed next to him. Squealing with a zeal to light the heart of any mother, he feasts and rolls away from the light. Still . . .

Even a blind cat will stumble onto a mouse, save of course, if the room is locked and sealed. Bingo! Isolated and insulated who, then, will see–it–when yet another surfer arrives this very eve, when the silver beam slides in like so many shooting stars, the chances never end, never weary of tempting us. Reverse it all for a moment, ride the opposing wave, catch the Silver Surfer, what possible damage could be done?

I logged onto to the City Government website, looked up the unclaimed bodies, all the John and Jane Does, and there was Felix.. Fred, I guess as a joke, or favor, put Felix in quotes next to the last entry. John Doe "Felix" 8/30/2009, was just one among about eighty or ninety listed over the last two hundred years.

Dad once told me when I was seven, "Son, every man has a storm raging inside of him and . . . let me see how can I put this . . . without the manners and decorum of a civilized people the chaos that would ensue of inviting oneself into another's rage would be untenable." My knitted brow was his next cue, "OK . . . try this, son: speak when you are spoken to."

And so gods and saints, prophets and redeemers are folded into the white noise we generate to shield ourselves from life, leading Felix to riff even more,

A heater jumps. Nope, you won't see it, not a good one. Just the pop of the catcher's mitt is the only proof you'll have that the man on the mound threw the pitch. But buried inside that pitch is the only way man ever approaches any real participation in the speed of light. And when you do approach that sacred speed the universe slows to accept the limited confines of our reason.

Saw it myself one day . . . well twilight, on the steps of the courthouse. Low light clawing around the roofs and edges of the granite and glass like a big tom cat flexing his paws tryin' to get a good, firm grip. Then one set of eyes–gray-green– sparkling like marbles in the ocean surf, then another and another started hovering over me. I guess they all thought I was dead, checkin' to see if I was still breathin'.

"When I looked up at all the faces and eyes, I saw the light start to curl and jump off every window, fender, flagpole, streetlamp, anything with a glint or a shine to it.

Boom–gone–no light, a thundercloud as black as used motor oil blocked the sun.

One errant drop then another of rain started to fall while only a block away there was a deluge. Like some cartoon it continued to drop just a few pops of water on me, while a hundred feet away it was a solid curtain of rain. That's when it started.

In and around and through that thunderhead buckshot points of light burst through so that each droplet coming down on me was paired with its own ray of light. Made the raindrops hover and pause; turned each to a little crystal before hitting the concrete and painting it white-gold. And every set of eyes that had come over to check on me was transfixed, scared stiff to move and tied to the light and the water and the crystals exploding in and around and on them. No one moved. I was the camera and they were the photograph.

The droplets continued to explode and more and more people stopped, sat down, looked up, put their hands out, held their eyes open to catch the crystal drops. That's when I saw him, the Silver Surfer, low and easy, cool as the other side of the pillow coming off a beam straight from the center of that thunderhead. Yes sir, it was him, 'cause everyone on those stairs pointed, just like that photo from Dallas when the shots rang out in '63.

Then it hit me. I have never pointed at anything or anyone with the wonder or terror that Felix described in his journal. Was Dad right? Do each of us have a storm, an uncontrollable rage roiling inside or is it just a cover for the fear we have that we will never be able to pierce through the shield of white noise that surrounds us? Was that why Dad angered so quickly and apologized so often? Why Felix could never keep a job, but somehow managed, and now after reading his notebook, I see, actually thrived. Do only a few of us pierce that veil of white noise? Are anger, frustration, even violence like the imperfect poem or poorly played sonata? Are they awkward calls to look up and see the surfer, the wave sliding down and around us almost daily? Then I read the last entry for what seemed like the hundredth time.

> *Ignore the light and water and sound and . . . touch of the wind at your peril. A star succeeds in tying the universe together simply by casting its light out into the void. No one will ever know its beginning or its end except the soul who feels each breeze and gust of the wind as though they were an open invitation to latch onto a wave and then ride it like a bandit!*

Einstein, Satchmo, Baudelaire, the Silver Surfer and . . . Felix. Who would have guessed?

{ 17 } 1ˢᵗ Place Short Story

Plywood Jesus

By W. Scott Thomason

Zax stood on the side of the nameless, numbered county road, squinting against the light of the late winter morning as he studied a crude figure painted on a sheet of plywood held up by a brace of two-by-fours. The body was shaped like a giant pear, wearing robes filled in with flat white house paint. The arms stretched to the knees, each with a lump for a hand. There were no feet; instead, the figure appeared to float on endless legs. The head was nearly square, crudely formed underneath a beard of black smudges. The skin was the common egg-shell paint found on the walls of any room anywhere. The only background was the weathered plywood. Beneath the figure in square white letters was written SOON.

"I sure as hell hope that's not what the real Jesus looks like," Dew hollered against the wind sweeping through the tobacco fields sur-rounding the highway. He waited by the truck fifteen feet back, slurping coffee from a yellowed Thermos. "But even so, that's what you came for."

Zax rubbed his palms together before pulling out his camera. Gallery owners always wanted plenty of pictures. Zax could see that this art was exactly what New York City buyers wanted: common materials, a quaint sensibility, and an echo of the primitive that filled the deal with a missionary's sense of accomplishment. He snapped away, the gray, winter North Carolina sky and empty fields adding the perfect background to what could be his big break.

"Dew, has anyone come to town asking about the signs? Outsiders, I mean."

"To my knowledge you're the first. And I'm not sure if you really count."

Zax grew up twenty miles down the road in Faith Rock. After college he went to New York City with dreams of being an artist, but had ended up working in galleries before trying to make a career out of buying and selling an ever-changing series of creative trends. Folk art was hot at the moment, and he knew that in the market the moment matters more than anything.

"How many more signs before we get to Harwick's place?"

Dew had stepped closer because of the wind. "A couple on this route, but he's got more at his house."

Zax had returned to meet King Harwick, a recluse who a few months earlier had begun leaving plywood paintings of Jesus throughout the county. Zax had called and written the artist for weeks without success. His family had left North Carolina a few years before, so he booked a flight from JFK to Greensboro and arranged a ride with Dew Vinson, the father of a childhood friend. Dew was an odd jobs repairman and one of the only people who interacted with Harwick. As a teenager Zax had found his own parents infuriating, but he had believed that Dew was the only level-headed adult on earth.

Inside of the aging Plymouth Arrow pickup, Zax realized he no longer recognized the shade of late winter brown covering the ground, the decade away having dulled his memory of the land. Art had seemed an escape when he lived here, but now he couldn't recall what from or where he believed it would take him. Dew interrupted his thoughts.

"So you really think you can get money for these signs?"

Zax held his breath for a moment. "His type of art is getting a good price right now. It's the right time for a guy like him." Zax needed to find a new talent in order to distinguish himself as a broker. It seemed that every southern folk artist had already been discovered, but the market wanted more.

Dew spoke again. "If anyone wants to buy what old King does then they just have too much money."

"I appreciate you letting me tag along, Dew." It was the fourth time Zax had thanked him since being picked up at the airport. "I don't want Harwick to be mad at you for bringing me around."

"Now you stop thanking me, son. Just don't do anything that King might blame me for. He's unlucky and he pays in full. A repairman's dream."

"I'm just going to make him a generous offer. I don't see how he would be offended by that."

Dew laughed low. "Whatever it is you're expecting, you're probably not going to get exactly that."

They continued down the road to Bement, a railroad hamlet that had slowly died after the opening of the interstate to the east. Main Street was lined by brick buildings with boarded up storefront windows, one still bearing the flaking, white shoe-polish of "Going Out of Business."

A plywood painting stood by the unused railroad tracks in the middle of town. The white robes of this figure were smudged, and the cheeks were slightly red, giving the face a hint of humanity Zax thought was missing in the previous piece. Long brown hair spilled over the shoulders, a touch lighter than the eyebrows that pinched down on the blue eyes that seemed to look past the observer. The lump hands were similar to those in the first painting, and again the legs ran endlessly into the plywood earth. Zax studied the figure's face and the message written in white at the bottom: BROKEN.

Zax rubbed his hand over the rough plywood face, and looked at how small his fingers appeared next to the crude, chunky head. As he felt the roughness of the eyes, he remembered the place where they stood. "Hey Dew - where's the Marilyn Monroe statue that used to be here?"

The statue and its story was a part of the county that Zax could remember. In the late nineteen fifties the Norfolk Southern Railroad hoped to compete with the developing interstate system by rechristening a stretch of track running through central North Carolina. They brought in Marilyn Monroe for ribbon cutting ceremonies in every town along the line. She was so drunk by the time her train got to Bement that no one would let her handle scissors. The mayor cut the ribbon, his hands placed over Marilyn's as she leaned into his chest. A Norfolk Southern man stood smiling behind them like the pose was both natural and intended. Marilyn blankly stared for pictures before sloppily swaying back onto the train. Bement immediately put up a fiberglass statue of her in hopes of attracting tourists. As the town began to die, the statue became a late night hangout for teenagers from Faith Rock. Zax hadn't thought of the statue in years.

"That statue has been gone a while," Dew said. "Not sure what happened to it. It might have fallen apart and gotten hauled off."

Zax thought it odd that the Marilyn statue could disappear, since the legend of her visit had seemed to be just as much a part of Bement as the railroad tracks, but he didn't want to look foolish.

"How well do you know Harwick?"

"As well as you can know anybody who only pays in cash. He leases his land to a neighboring farmer. He's been widowed for several years. He sold insurance, I think. I reckon he did alright."

"Does he call you when he needs something?"

"You know him long?"

"A few years. I never had much cause to come out this far until he called me. Not sure how he got my number. He's a weirdo for sure, but he's never done me any wrong."

Zax realized that he hadn't removed his fingers from the face of the plywood Jesus. "Is he going to preach at us?"

"Now, just because King paints Jesus signs doesn't mean he's some kind of preacher." Dew took a drink a coffee from the Thermos he had nursed all morning. "A man who's got to yell doesn't have much to say."

Zax lowered his hand. "Does he ever put Bible verses on them?"

"Not that he labels. Though what's on them might be in there somewhere."

"You read the Bible?" It wasn't the kind of question he would have asked years before.

Dew responded with an answer that he wouldn't have given a teenager. "No. I just go to church."

They returned to the truck after Zax had taken pictures. They saw two more paintings as they went further into the country, both similar to those before: dimensionless, plain, and potentially valuable to the folk-art thirsty galleries. As they neared Harwick's farm, Zax tried to commit to memory the sound of the country road passing beneath them before breaking his own silence.

"So Dew – you think Harwick's crazy?"

Dew laughed. "Of course he's crazy. If you thought the Messiah was returning, would you announce Him with plywood? If the Second Coming's not the time for the good lumber I don't know what is. Hell, splurge for some masonry."

*

Outside of King Harwick's farmhouse stood five plywood Jesus signs, congregated like dots on a domino. The figures were similar to the disproportionate and dimensionless paintings along the road, except the center Jesus elevated his left hand with the palm facing outward. Written in white on the base of the four outer paintings were FORGOTTEN, PREPARE, AGAIN, and RENEW. The base of the fifth sign read TODAY. Zax walked among the paintings as Dew pulled his toolbox from the back of the truck.

"He moves them around," Dew said. "Last time I was here they were in a line, blocking the driveway. I had to park in the grass."

"So no one thinks this is a little odd?"

"You boys used to never come out to the country to think."

Zax looked down at the ground and followed Dew to the porch. Both men wiped off their shoes on patchy outdoor carpet. Dew pounded on the door with a bulky fist as Zax rubbed his palms down his slacks. He rehearsed in his head how best to talk to a folk artist about a sale.

The door opened to reveal a short, stocky, bald-headed man. His scalp was speckled with age spots. His hands were fat and nubby, like the blobs in the paintings. He wore brown corduroy pants and a white Oxford shirt dotted with paint spots, some old and some fresh. Zax was disappointed that Harwick didn't have an unkempt beard or long hair – buyers loved those – but he still thought that the artist's picture would look great on an exhibition advertisement.

Dew nodded his head. "Howdy, King. Just here to see what needs fixing. This here's Zax Lucas, an old friend of my boy's. He says he might want to buy some of your art."

Zax cringed at the introduction. He extended his hand, hoping that Dew's earnestness hadn't ruined the deal before he had a chance to speak. "Hello, Mr. Harwick. I'm Zaxby Lucas, and I would like to talk to you about finding a wider audience for your work."

Harwick cupped Zax's entire hand in his but did not shake. He looked Zax in the eye. "I already have my audience, Mr. Lucas." He turned to Dew. "The downstairs toilet is clogged and the plunger doesn't work." Dew sighed at the announcement. "There's also some lifting I'll need your help with when you're done."

Harwick released Zax's hand and walked back into the house. Dew followed and motioned Zax along. Once inside Dew nodded and stepped into a hallway on the side of the house, leaving Zax in the front room with Harwick. The walls were decorated with rusted and chipped scythes, rakes, and pitchforks. These were real, and not the decorative tools with black metal blades and red wooden handles that hung in many of the area houses that Zax had visited as a child. Harwick moved slowly towards the rear of the room. He patted a stack of letters on a half-empty bookshelf. "A shame you came all the way down here."

Zax pretended to admire a scythe. "It's not a problem at all, sir. I grew up over in Faith Rock –"

"I figured as much, seeing as Dew said you knew his son."

Zax tried to move the conversation towards the sale. "Mr. Harwick, there is a growing market for the type of art that you produce. A lot –"

"And what is that?"

"Excuse me, sir?"

"What type is that?"

"It's called folk art. It is a widely respected – "

Harwick interrupted him by raising an index finger. "What makes you any different from an encyclopedia salesman?" He pointed to the bookshelves. "I don't have any encyclopedias." He turned and walked further into the house. Zax paused, then followed. He passed through a plain kitchen and into a long hallway that smelled of paint. Harwick headed towards an enclosed porch at the rear of the house.

The porch was a studio. A gray tarp lined the floor. The windows were open despite the late winter chill. A new plywood painting stood in the center of the room. The swirled robes were tinted with a bright blue, and the cheeks shone full in the indoor light. The figure's blue eyes matched the robes, and seemed to look past Zax. Cans of open house paint and wet brushes sat on a metal worktable, its uncovered top a multi-colored pox. Harwick dipped a brush in a can of red, knelt down in front of the plywood, and began to paint uneven box letters beneath the figure.

Zax pulled his camera from his bag. Gallery owners often wanted photographs of artists working. "Don't take my picture," Harwick said without stopping.

"Sometimes audiences are interested in seeing how an artist works."

Harwick looked up. "My audience has greater things to consider."

Zax lowered the camera. He knew that the most important part of a negotiation was to keep the artist talking.

"Sir, I would like to discuss buying some of your paintings. You wouldn't have to go to New York. I'll represent you to galleries and private buyers. We can handle everything here. You'll never have to go anywhere." He understood that folk artists tended to dislike the attention given at exhibitions.

"You seem to think that people would want to buy my art."

It was a familiar response. "Most people who collect aren't creative. They find great joy in the creativity of others. Some people say it's because they want to be creative themselves, but I think the creativity of others helps them see the world in a way they otherwise couldn't."

"And you think my work would do that?"

"I do. Your painting isn't constrained by traditional boundaries, which is something else collectors are looking for right now." Zax felt that the conversation was developing as it should.

Harwick spoke as he continued to paint. "I'm not concerned with right now."

"Art has a strange way of communicating things to people. You never know what message your work might send to someone."

"I know my message."

"Displaying your art in a gallery will allow more people to receive that message."

Harwick lifted his brush from the base of the plywood and looked up towards Zax.

"Do you believe, Mr. Lucas?"

Zax was not sure how to answer, but he needed to keep Harwick talking. He took a short breath. "I went to church while growing up."

"Church?" Harwick pointed the brush towards Zax. "Churches see God in the way that they want to see Him. Their belief in God becomes their god." He stood up and wiped his hands on a scrap of cloth. "But I believe in God the way He wants me to believe." He turned to the table and dipped his brush into the can. "If Jesus Himself came back down today and told people of their folly, they would not listen. They would tell Him, *You are not God.* And they would believe it." Harwick kneeled again and resumed painting the letters. "You have to know why you believe as much as what you believe, Mr. Lucas."

Zax cleared his throat. "Why have you changed to red, sir? The letters, I mean. They're now in red. Your other signs are in white."

Harwick stopped his work. "It's nearing Easter, isn't it, Mr. Lucas? The blood of the Cross. I'm sure you heard about that in church."

"I like the change, sir. The red contrasts beautifully with the blue."

Harwick stood up and rested his brush on the table. He faced Zax and pointed towards the Jesus painting. "Where is the art here, Mr. Lucas?"

Zax had thought out his answer. "In the materials. There's an inner beauty in the simplicity of the plywood, I believe." That line always did well in reviews.

"That's what you believe, Mr. Lucas?"

Zax breathed in the paint smell filling the room. "Why not use a higher quality of wood – for God's glory?"

"Now that's a question a good church person would ask. A deacon maybe, or even a preacher." He stood up. "So if one asks, I'll tell them for the inner beauty of its simplicity." Harwick dipped his brush into the red and resumed painting.

Zax squeezed his hands together, noticing the wetness on his palms. He watched Harwick paint, unable to come up with a way to redirect the conversation. When Harwick finished he stood up and approached Zax.

"So why did you stop believing, Mr. Lucas?"

Zax was confused. "I just stopped going to church, I guess –"

"No, Mr. Lucas." He held up the brush dripping red. "In this."

Zax watched some of the paint run onto the top of Harwick's shoes before saying, "I still believe in art."

"'I believe in art.'" Harwick waved his brush towards the plywood Jesus. Wet paint splattered onto the figure's robes and dripped onto the floor. "There's some right there."

Zax paused before answering. "I mean art more as an abstract."

"I paint. You buy. There's nothing abstract about that difference." He turned towards the painting, and then pointed his brush towards the plywood. "Where is the art here, Mr. Lucas?"

Zax looked at the figure staring past him. He tried to think of past deals and his training, and what he should say to keep the conversation moving as it should, but instead he thought of how it felt to paint himself. "The art is in the eyes. In all of them. It's the eyes."

"Is it now?" Harwick picked up his brush. He again knelt before the figure and resumed working on the letters. Zax thought about what he should say next when Dew stepped quietly onto the covered porch and placed a hand on his shoulder. Zax startled, and hoped Harwick had not noticed him flinch. Dew looked at the artist like he was about to scold a child. He held out a handful of miniature army men that were originally green but were now coated in a mix of bright paint and pipe-soaked sludge.

"King, I had to take that toilet off the floor. These were in the trap."

Harwick continued painting. "Do you think those were the cause of the clog, Dew?"

"Think? I don't have to think. It's a known fact that the plumbing isn't for flushing away pieces of junk."

"I always trust that you can fix whatever breaks."

"I appreciate your faith, but we've had this conversation before. You can't flush plastic figures down the toilet. Or brushes, balled up newspaper, rubber bands, any size screw, or those little cups that come on the top of Pepto-Bismol."

Harwick continued to paint. "Those things failed."

"I don't know what that means, King." Dew took a deep breath and leaned against the door frame. "I'm not a magician. If you keep this up you are going to seriously damage your system to where I can't fix it."

He pointed a thumb towards Zax. "You'll have to sell him all of your paintings to cover the repairs."

"Thank you for the candor, Dew. I appreciate your honesty."

Dew looked at Zax and shook his head before speaking to Harwick again. "Now you said you needed help moving something."

"Yes, in the barn."

"Well, I believe old Zax would be glad to pitch in." Dew patted Zax on the back and let out his low laugh. Harwick rose up from the plywood and walked towards the back door, exposing the word REDEEM.

Harwick opened the screen door and headed down the brick stairs. The yard had surrendered to dark clover, and a line of sunken concrete steppingstones led to a peeling wooden barn behind the house. The barn smelled of paint and damp winter earth. Inside were dozens of pieces of plywood secured against warping in long metal braces. In the middle stood a Jesus painting different from the previous figures. The skin was well-shaded, giving the face a more human appearance. The hair was not black but a bright silvery white. The white eyebrows were sharply angled downward towards the nose. The figure was aligned towards the left side of the plywood. The smudged, hovering robes were a fiery red, a mix of deep and light shades. The long arms stretched towards the right side of the board, in an embrace of something that was not there. The Jesus was complete except for two circles of bare plywood in place of the eyes, and no message.

Beside the figure was a metal table holding paints and brushes. Harwick opened a can of black and began stirring. "What I need you to move is over there in the corner." He pointed to a man-sized object covered by a green tarp standing in the back of the barn, barely lit by the daylight leaking in through the loft. "It needs to be brought here."

Zax and Dew crossed the floor. Zax looked back to see Harwick staring at the painting.

"I thought you said he wasn't going to preach, Dew."

"I said he didn't have to yell. And I wouldn't call what old King does preaching. He just thinks out loud a lot more than most folks."

Zax looked at Harwick before leaning in closer to Dew. "I don't think he's going to sell anything."

"Not everybody is interested in being part of the big time." Dew reached over the object and pulled off the tarp, revealing the statue of Marilyn Monroe from Bement Park. "Well," Dew said, wiping dust from his hands. "Here's your answer to where this went."

The statue was a fiberglass replica of Marilyn's scene in the *Seven Year Itch* where her white dress is blown over her head by a blast of air from a subway grate. The statue may have looked life-like at one point, but the weathered piece before them was more like Zax remembered. The once-blonde hair was chipped and faded. The flawless face was cracked. The elevated edges of the dress were broken off in chunks, leaving the perimeter sharp and jagged.

The wear was still apparent on Marilyn's skin and dress through the layer of semi-translucent red paint that now covered her. The base of the statue was originally corrugated to represent the subway venting, but most of it was gone, leaving only remnants of the grate around her feet. White vertical block letters had been added across the chest, spelling BROKEN.

"Just like the Jesus in the park," Zax said.

"Huh?"

"Like in the park, the painting in Bement – Dew, should we take this over to him? I mean, isn't this stolen property?"

"No one seems to have thought about the old girl in a long time. And we don't know if it's stolen. It's just not a part of that place anymore."

Zax looked back towards Harwick standing before the Jesus painting. "It seems wrong to let him mess up something that once mattered to people."

Dew looked around Marilyn's face. "I thought you considered what King does to be art."

The statue weighed about sixty pounds, and was easy enough for two men to carry across the barn. Dew tilted the head towards Zax, who studied the face in his hands before lifting his end.

"He asked me if I believe in art. I'm not sure what to say to that."

"Well, do you?"

"Of course I do. But I don't think Harwick believes me."

Dew raised Marilyn's fractured base. "Seems all you have to do is change his mind." He laughed to himself as they began to move towards the front of the barn. Zax was silent, watching the floor as they carried the statue to the plywood painting. The transparent red coat covering Marilyn began to flake off in their hands.

"Lean it there," Harwick said when they reached him, pointing to the space besides the plywood Jesus. From underneath the table he pulled out an old electric drill, fitted with a one inch boring bit. On the table sat a large metal bolt.

Zax looked at Harwick. "The paint is coming off this statue. It needs scraping and priming before you do anything else. A gesso, probably."

"I'm not worried about the paint, Mr. Lucas."

"It won't last outside, sir."

"Nothing lasts, Mr. Lucas."

When the statue was in place Harwick pressed the bit into Marilyn's stomach. Zax shook his head and moved forward, but Dew put his hand on Zax's shoulder before stepping towards the artist. "King, you may want to use a small bit first on this thing. Make you a pilot hole. The one you have in there is likely to skip out of that fiberglass."

Harwick raised his palm towards Dew. "Thank you for the advice." He held the drill in his right hand and pressed his left against the statue, his thumb and forefinger making a crescent around the bit.

Dew put his hand on Harwick's shoulder. "I wouldn't hold it that way, King."

The artist brushed off Dew's hand without a word and started the drill. Dust from the fiberglass stomach rose from the bit as the red-painted skin gave way. Zax squinted as the drill bore into the statue. He tried to remember what it had looked like a decade before when it was still in the park, covered in black grime and thin lines of mildew. He pictured himself and E.P. Vinson cradling beer bottles in the hands pressing the dress against the subway blast as the cracked face smiled and looked away.

The drill began to shake. The bit jerked out of the hole, the motor stopping with a sound like the ripping of weak cloth. The drill fell to the floor as the artist clutched his hand to his chest, a line of blood dripping between his fingers. Instead of a scream he let out three short groans.

Dew eased Harwick to the ground and sat him against the wall. Zax grabbed a scrap towel from the table and pressed it onto the wound, wrapping his hand around Harwick's. The bit had torn away a ring of flesh from the left palm.

"What'd I tell you," Dew said. "How bad you think it is, King?"

"Cut. Just cut."

Zax continued to press against the palm. "We ought to take you to get stitches."

"Nonsense. The work has to be finished."

"You won't be doing that for a while," Zax said. He looked to Dew. "Can you bring the truck around here?"

Harwick squeezed his fingers around Zax's hand. "I'm not going anywhere until the work is finished."

Dew stood up and laughed low. "Well King, you're not touching tools with that hand. And I prefer to paint with a sprayer."

King closed his eyes and drew in a long breath. "Mr. Lucas is going to finish it."

"Me?" Zax applied more pressure to the wound, blood soaking through the cloth and sticking to his fingers. "This isn't my art, sir. I only came here to make an offer on some of your pieces."

Harwick winced. "It has to be finished."

Zax looked at Dew, who reached over and took Harwick's hand. "It's what you came back for, isn't it?"

Zax stood up and studied the red paint that sloppily covered Marilyn's chipped and cracked surface. He looked at the partial hole cut into the stomach, and then glanced down at Harwick. Zax picked up the drill. Spots of Harwick's blood shone through the fiberglass dust and particles of red paint stuck to the bit. He paused, and then returned the drill to the table. He stared at the blind plywood Jesus, whose arms were lined up to wrap around the shoulders of the Hollywood star.

He grabbed a brush from the table. The wood was cold from the late winter, but the handle felt familiar against his soft fingers. He studied the black paint that was open before him, and pushed it aside.

Zax opened cans of red and blue and poured half of each onto the bare table, the excess running onto the floor and his shoes. He mixed the paints together into a purple. He swirled in his brush and painted the color over the block letters running across Marilyn's chest.

Zax put down the purple brush and opened a can of white. He poured it onto the mix, blending the colors into a deep gray. Zax smoothed out the paint on the end of his brush against the corner of the table, and gently dabbed the eyes into the face of the Jesus, the color slowly darkening against the plain wood. He picked up the purple brush and wrote above the figure, SEE.

Zax stepped back and leaned into the wall of the barn. He squinted against the winter light shining in on the figures. Harwick stood up beside him.

"So, Mr. Lucas, do you believe?"

{ 18 } 2nd Place Short Story

Their Crazy

by Susannah Cecil

There's this puzzle I've been worryin' over, and could I run it by you while we wait? See, my Mama said every family has at least one crazy, but I'm not so sure. She said our family's was Cousin Liddy, the girl who looked at you with one eye while the other one looked off to the left, like it was watching a plane take off or somethin'. Truth is, I never did feel right around Liddy. Turns out I had a pretty good gut, too, 'cause she's the one what turned up dead "*by her own hand.*" Or so they said.

Mama says nobody but a crazy person would do somethin' such as that. "You'd have to be crazy to take your own life," Mama said. But they say Liddy did; so there you go. Then there was Cousin Jimmy's wife Sheila; the woman that his Mama, my Aunt Belle…my Daddy's sister…did *not* want Jimmy to marry.

"That girl's gonna be the albatross around your neck, son," Aunt Belle would holler, standin' at her ironing board. "She'll drag you down, and you won't ever see that college you're so hep on goin' off to!"

Every Tuesday was ironing day for my Mama and Aunt Belle. They'd do their ironing in Aunt Belle's kitchen, because she had the best ironing board, lots of room across her kitchen table. Cousin Jimmy would sit at the corner of that table before work, crisp white sheets stacked in neat rows, underwear mounted up on wings like eagles. He'd sit there eating grits and eggs, listening to Aunt Belle run-down his latest girl. He never did say much of nothin' back to her; just snuffled those eggs down, nodded into his coffee, then asked for more sausage whenever she took a breath.

I wasn't in big-school yet, so Mama'd take me with her to Aunt Belle's. I used to sit under that ironing board with my army men, pretending we were on spy missions in Iraq. We'd radio back to Base, "Code words: girl - albatross. Over..." Jimmy married Sheila two months later anyway. Then they moved in with Aunt Belle's husband, my Uncle Jeff, in that house on the hill.

When I asked Mama about it, she said, "You see, Jike? Jimmy changed his mind about college; decided to get married instead, and soon they'll bring us a new little cousin. Isn't that nice?" Yeah. Real nice, I guess. Only Aunt Belle didn't think so. She kept steaming out new code words on Tuesday mornings.

Turns out Cousin Sheila was nice enough, but she went right to work getting' fat, and Aunt Belle would say she was a sieve and a trollop. "How can I go on, with my son's offspring being launched into this world by a trollop?" she'd moan at Mama.

It seemed to me she'd want her grandbaby to pony-trollop into town like Jesus did, but I wasn't sure about launchin' offsprings. I radioed out, "All clear to launch – sieve and trollop – over."

By the time that baby was born (without the launching, thank the good Lord in heaven), Aunt Belle was wound up like a June bug tied to dental floss. There was nothin' Uncle Jeff could do against it, so he just went back to his house while Aunt Belle hollered, "Go on, then! If a husband can't stand by his wife in hard times, then he should leave! By hellfire and damnation, that baby will be raised in a good home - my home! That trollop will ruin him in six months time, and I'll not stand for it!"

By then, see, our Tuesday ironing was switched to Saturdays, because Mama went for a job at the Mill. Cousin Sheila went too, so she could carry her own weight . . . which was considerable less than it had been. So, it didn't seem to me she had all that much weight to carry. But what did I know? And I needed to tend my own business anyway.

After that, Sheila's baby James and me stayed with Aunt Belle through the weekdays. But no more army men for me, on account of Aunt Belle, "Jike, you'll not scatter those green plastic things here anymore. I'll step on those damned sharp edges and pierce my feet like Jesus on the cross. And don't you know? Baby James'll choke on 'em as quick as you can say 'Lee Harvey Oswald'."

So, I made do with the Lincoln Logs from the junk-drawer, and the one-armed G.I. Joe that Roscoe buried in the red dirt last summer. Mornings would still bring Cousin Jimmy down the hill, totin' Baby James. Jimmy would sit at Aunt Belle's same kitchen table eating breakfast, listening to her squall about his wife, while she spooned mashed bananas into the baby's mouth. I'd radio to Base, "Green plastic threatens General Belle; Lee Harvey chokes on baby bananas. Over."

Here lately -- I'm gettin' to my point about what's puzzlin' me, see? -- I asked Mama about Cousin Liddy, and was she truly crazy like Aunt Belle said? Or was she just sad, sad, sad because she stayed with Aunt Belle all the time? After Mama popped my mouth for disrespectin' my elders, she slumped against our refrigerator and slid to the floor like a bear scratchin' his back. Then she busted out in tears, only I couldn't see 'em, 'cause her face was all smushed into the dish towel she was holding. When she stopped 'haw, haw, haw-ing' into the towel, Mama took a deep breath and looked me straight between the eyes.

"That was a bad, sad time, Jikey. Maybe you don't remember it much, you were so little, only four I think, and your Daddy had just got sent off. But cousin Liddy was 17. She was always stuck to Aunt Belle's hip, doing just what she said, and when. She didn't even jump, lest Aunt Belle said so. Time came, though, that Liddy found herself a bit of spine and started seein' this fella over at Badin Lake. When Aunt Belle found out, she threw so much sand, we couldn't see clear for miles. It was pretty soon after that, Cousin Jimmy found Liddy hanging from the rafters in the back of the barn. He flew into a panic, grabbed the first knife he could find and raced to cut her down."

I asked Mama what was the panic, and why Jimmy grabbed a knife; and wouldn't Liddy just've hung on until she lost her grip and let go anyway? I mean, GI Joe's only got one arm, and *even he* could hang from the rafters for a good 10 minutes. Then, Mama 'haw, haw, haw-ed' into her towel again, and looked up to Jesus all puffy-eyed. She prayed somethin' about Liddy's soft backbone, her roamy eye, and Aunt Belle's hard heart. She cried that she's got to find a way outta here, but she didn't want to be blamed for breaking the family tree, and how she ain't got nowhere else to go anyway. She cried about won't Jesus ever hear her prayers?

After that, she 'haw, haw, haw-ed' some more into that raggedy towel, and I patted and rubbed her shoulder until just before supper time, which didn't matter by then, 'cause my gut felt like a big ball of cement anyway. Then Mama breathed real hard, blew her nose good, lifted her eyes and said, "How 'bout you go wash up now, baby? Go on. Everything'll be alright."

And I said, "Yes ma'am I will." So I left her there, went and washed both my hands, and G.I. Joe's one. Then me and him squatted under the bathroom sink to call for back-up, because we sure needed it, "Come in Green Unit back-up. Special agent Liddy lost grip on rafters 'by her own hand' and turned up dead. Captain Mama sends distress signals. Need back-up pronto! Over."

Like I said, I didn't feel much like supper that night. So me and GI Joe stayed under the sink for a good while, until Uncle Jeff knocked on the door and said to come out; said our undercover duty was over.

And that's how come we're waitin' here at the bus station, 'cause my Daddy finally got home from his middle-east, and Mama says we're moving to Montana – except I think it's really just Rowan County. They said big skies and real horses, and Daddy says we're gonna live by a Dude Ranch – only I think it's just a dairy farm. But Daddy also said I can bring all the army men I want, so me and GI Joe's been making big plans!

And this is what I wanted to run by you: Mama said every family has their crazy, and ours was Cousin Liddy. But my Daddy says that's hogwash, and Cousin Liddy was 'just the snoot on that old hound dog.' So I wonder, which one of them do you reckon is closer to right?

Yep. That's kinda what I thought. . . Me neither.

{ 19 } 3rd Place Short Story

Hurricane Season

By Hampton Williams Hofer

Cramming into the backseat of your neighbors' minivan during a midnight evacuation is not as miserable as it may sound, not if you're fifteen and in love with their lanky French exchange student Gaspard, whose arm is touching your arm in the dark. You can't see much out of the windows, apart from the red glow of taillights running in streaks of rain. The view through the sunroof is so inky and empty that you may be looking at the bottom of a rooftop cargo case. Gaspard is tense and unmoving beside you, the fabric of his sleeve something posh and Parisian like acrylic cashmere. The rain hits the van from the side, as if little boys were lining the streets with water guns, the way they do during the 4th of July parade. When the roar of the wind picks up, your mind flits to the black-and-white image of Dorothy and Toto. You picture your own house – a shingled bungalow, paint peeling off the window frames that face the ocean – spinning into the storm. But that was a tornado, and this is a hurricane. Two hurricanes. You figure Gaspard didn't imagine this when he signed up to spend his fall semester in Port St. Pete. He's been living with your neighbors the Erikssons for six weeks. You've loved him for at least four.

The first of the hurricanes, named Philippe, developed as a tropical storm off the coast of Africa, swirling its way toward the Caribbean. The second, Roxanne, caught up to Philippe near western Cuba, the two storms turning northwest into the Gulf of Mexico bound for Port St. Pete. They weren't supposed to hit until tomorrow night. Your Earth Science teacher had explained the difference between tropical storms and hurricanes, something to do with the speed of the winds and the height of the swells. All you remember is that the system for naming storms is alphabetical: Arlene, Barry, Christopher, and so on, but they skip the letter Q. After Philippe came Roxanne. You feel left out, because your name is Quinn. You'll never be a hurricane.

Mrs. Eriksson is driving, inching forward through sheets of rain, chatting in whispers to your mother in the front seat. Your father and Mr. Eriksson are still sandbagging the doors to the garage you share – they sent the women and children ahead like some scene from *Titanic*. You are all heading to your aunt's house in Montgomery, a few hours northwest: far enough to be safe from the storm, and close enough for a quick return. Your Aunt Louise invented the first line of silicon gadget covers for cellphones and tablets, and her house is plenty big for everyone. She lives there alone with her slew of golden retrievers and horses and a teacup pig that was supposed to grow no larger than fifty pounds but now tips the scales at three hundred and has to live in the barn. You're hoping Aunt Louise won't get too drunk in front of Gaspard and dance to Gwen Stefani by the pool in her t-shirt and underwear like you've seen her do before.

Sitting behind Mrs. Eriksson in one of the bucket seats is her sixteen-year-old son Drew. In the other is Drew's little sister, asleep in a bulky car seat. Drew gets car sick in the way back, so he says. You ended up in the middle of the back row, a position widely known as the least desirable, and you did enough huffing and sighing to conceal the heat in your cheeks and thump in your chest when you realized you'd be in such close proximity to Gaspard. On your other side is your younger brother Michael whose arm is also touching yours, though you keep elbowing him away. He doesn't even whisper when he turns to you and asks if you think everyone is going to die.

The bridge that connects Port St. Pete to the mainland of Florida is narrow and low, used as much for fishing as driving. Now it is as crowded as you have ever seen it, both lanes going in one direction: out. The severe weather sirens are pounding through the town behind you. You can hear them through the rain, shrill and echoing among the empty houses and the boardwalk, your school with its darkened hallways and abandoned desks. You like the rain, the clouds. You've been conditioned that way. Your father owns a sandy-floored restaurant called the Shrimp Shack with a faux thatched roof and a chalkboard advertising the weekly drink specials. Your mother sells her handmade seashell jewelry in a little booth by the hostess stand. Rain brings business: people fleeing the beach with their soggy towels, or growing restless in their rental homes, sick of board games that are missing half the pieces. They want battered shrimp and shell necklaces in order to feel like they're still on vacation. Bad weather is good for the townies. You like the rain, but this rain already feels different. You have the vague feeling of being in the two-dollar car wash behind the Exxon station.

No, you tell Michael, obviously you don't think anyone is going to die. You throw in a little laugh in hopes of making Gaspard relax. But what if the two storms converge, Michael wants to know. What if Philippe and Roxanne become one super-hurricane? Drew turns around in his seat and tells Michael it isn't possible. Drew says the two storms are using the same water. It's like two people trying to live off of one heart. The heart can pump and pump, keeping both people alive for a while, but eventually one of them will prevail at the sake of the other.

You all consider the analogy. Yes, says Gaspard, but now zee remaining person is stronger, no?

You've been sitting behind Gaspard in Chemistry for five weeks, during which time the perfectly manicured hairline at the base of his neck has grown shaggy, dark curls now brushing his collar. Apparently in France they do their sciences in a different order, so Gaspard has already taken physics, which is what the rest of the juniors at Port St. Pete High School are taking. Gaspard has to spend the semester with you and the sophomores in Chemistry, learning the atomic structures and colligative properties of acids and bases from a redheaded student teacher named Mr. Casey whose lisp makes him nearly impossible to understand, even with English as a first language. Twice Gaspard has come over to your house for help with the Chemistry homework. The first time, he arrived unannounced at the front door with the strap of his leather satchel pinning his shirt tightly to his narrow chest. All of the other guys you knew carried nylon backpacks. Gaspard had a stubby, foreign-looking pencil tucked behind one ear. You had been sitting at the kitchen table, just out of the shower with your hair still damp around your shoulders, wearing – humiliatingly – your pajamas, even though it was hardly past seven. He had furrowed his thick brow and twirled his pencil around one of the curls at the nape of his neck as you showed him how to complete the chart on ionic and covalent bonds.

Mrs. Eriksson turns the radio volume up just loud enough for you to hear the broadcaster from the local soft rock station. He tells everyone to be careful, wishing you good luck and assuring you all that the traffic will lighten up after the bridge, which you've just entered at last. Then his voice fades away into the opening chords of *Roxanne* by the Police. The mothers laugh when they recognize the song. *Roxanne*, Sting croaks, *you don't have to put on the red light.* Gaspard hums along but just barely, such that he might not even know he's doing it. Without turning toward him, you ask if he likes Sting. This song I like, he says, but is about a prostitute.

The sirens woke you before your mother came in flicking on the overhead in your bedroom. You were in your new pajamas, a fitted tank top with matching little striped boxer shorts. You had bought them after your first homework session with Gaspard, unwilling to be caught again in your faded and pilly flannel pants. You were already packed to leave town, as most residents of Port St. Pete were planning to head inland the next day before the hurricanes were sure to hit. But then the weathermen and politicians, always with a flare for the dramatic, decided to mandate the evacuation tonight since it seemed Roxanne was gaining speed. She's still only a category two, but you know why they're being especially cautious. Last year, Stanley Wiggins was killed during a category two when the Exxon sign – which had been leaning for some time – crashed through his windshield. You heard at school that the sign landed at such a precise angle that the corner of the "N" cleanly impaled Stanley. Your father said when something like that happens, it means your number is up.

The sirens, like the politicians, seem a bit dramatic, reminiscent of a time before televisions and cell phone alerts. You had slid into a pair of jean shorts and brushed your hair, but there had not been time for much else in the way of making yourself presentable. You console yourself with the fact that it is dark in the back seat anyway, your faces lit only by the red glow of brake lights all around you. You can tell that Gaspard, too, was woken up and hurried to the car. There is a line on his cheek from a pillowcase's crease. You imagine him sleeping on his stomach, mouth open, face pressed to the pillow, and you wonder if he drools.

He starts when someone raps on Mrs. Eriksson's window. She rolls it down just slightly, rain already streaking the inside of her door as

Coach Shapiro's voice fills the car. Someone's stuck down at the end of the bridge, he says, that's what's making the backup so bad. He's holding a flashlight and wearing some sort of waxy poncho, from what you can see. He's heading back to his house on foot to get some extra batteries. One of only two physical educators at Port St. Pete High, he coaches at least five sports, soccer among them. The first time Coach Shapiro saw Gaspard juggling a soccer ball in second period gym, all tall and lean with those defined calf muscles, Coach Shapiro had tried to convince everyone to keep the French exchange student here through the spring season. But Gaspard would be gone in the spring. Drew would be gone too, his turn of the exchange, attending Gaspard's school in a small town called Cassel in the north of France. You looked it up and it turns out people have been living there since the Roman times. Some famous battle took place in Cassel in the year 10-something, a good seven centuries before Thomas Jefferson even thought about putting quill to scroll. Mrs. Eriksson thanks Coach Shapiro for the update and wipes the wet half of the steering wheel with her sleeve.

Drew turns around with an open bag of Doritos and offers you one. You're fine, thanks, but Gaspard accepts. He bites into his chips delicately, then wipes the seasoning from his fingers on his shorts instead of licking them like Drew does. You are halfway over the bridge when a clap of thunder rolls over the top of the van. It echoes in your ears, and you realize you have braced yourself against the seat as if thunder is something more than just noise. You feel silly. The hurricane isn't even hitting yet. Hurri*canes*.

Your mother turns around. She can't believe Drew's little sister is still asleep. With a fake smile plastered on her face, the kind that doesn't wrinkle her eyes, she asks if everyone is doing all right. You don't even give a grunt in response like Michael does, because all you know is that Gaspard's knee is somehow now touching yours. It wasn't before the thunder, and now it is. His shorts are navy and fitted, straight and simple – you noticed them in Chemistry. His knee is knobbier than yours. Unlike your arms, separated by the fabric of his long-sleeved shirt, this is skin-on-skin. And all at once, a dime-sized area on the side of your left knee is the only part of your body that matters at all.

The roar of the wind is worse on the bridge, and the cars seem to have stopped inching along. It's a movable bridge, the kind that opens for tall boats and barges. Everything is concrete until you reach the thick middle strip, a drawbridge made of metal. The tires sound different when they hit that part. The Erikssons' van is sandwiched between the cars piled up behind you and the ones stuck in front. Occasionally, a flash of lightening interrupts the darkness, lighting the water out over the inlet. It's beautiful, the way the sky opens up, and you almost say so.

Your mother mistakes your silence for fear or worry. It's all going to be fine, you guys. Dad will be right behind us, she says, these evacuations are an extreme precaution – I'm sure we'll return to find the house exactly as we left it. Mrs. Eriksson confirms. You're not worried about Port St. Pete. You know that it's a tough town, already on its third life, although you're a little hazy on the specifics, which are these: the oyster harvesters and shrimpers who founded the original village first came here in 1830, but a yellow fever epidemic wiped out almost everyone, and those who survived fled. The oyster harvesters came back before too long, and the settlement grew pretty big until Hurricane Henrietta tore everything up, right at the turn of the century. With new railroads and highways, Port St. Pete started its third life, right at the place where U.S. Highway 98 nearly dips into the Gulf of Mexico. You can't be positive about the chronology. But you know that no matter what happens, the shrimpers always come back.

Mrs. Eriksson cracks her window again, this time not for Coach Shapiro but for a police officer you don't recognize. It's flooded at the base of the bridge, he says. You know the place, where the road dips down before climbing back up and leveling out in a clean straight line towards Alabama. The officer says the water has risen so high across that little strip that only the tallest trucks can get through. Your mother is leaning forward in her seat. Cars have pulled over to the wide concrete shoulders of the bridge, though there is no room to turn around. You understand what's happening, because this has happened before during an especially rainy few days one spring when you were little. It didn't matter so much then – all it meant was that your mother couldn't make it out of Port St. Pete to a jewelry show in Apalachicola. Now it means something different, though you aren't sure what. Your van will be too low to cross, the officer is saying. Marty Tucker's Buick is stuck halfway in, can barely see his taillights under the water.

The second time Gaspard came over to do Chemistry homework, you were dressed in regular clothes, sitting on the soft leather couch in the den watching a rerun of *E! News*. He sat down beside you, a full seat cushion away. You had already finished the worksheet on the electronic structure of atoms, and you told him with practiced nonchalance that he could just copy yours. He had raised his thick brows at you: really, is okay? You shrugged your shoulders as if the worksheet hadn't taken you the better part of two hours, as if you could not care less about lispy, red-headed Mr. Casey and what his repercussions might be. When Gaspard had finished copying, he sat and watched with you. Americans and zare celebrities, he shook his head and flashed you a big-toothed smile. You could hear Michael and your parents in the kitchen running the water and chatting and closing cabinets. You wished they would disappear, wondered if Gaspard might have sat on the cushion right next to you if they did.

Your mother and Mrs. Eriksson are both on their cell phones talking to their husbands. Your father has a truck, but he can't get it anywhere near the bridge. Michael is quiet for once, and even Drew has quit chomping on his Doritos in order to try and hear what Mr. Eriksson is saying on the other end of the line. Gaspard didn't follow all that the policeman had said. He turns to you now and whispers, there is no other bridge? You shake your head, a serious and grim look on your face, despite the fact that you are more excited than afraid. No one is taking out a boat in this weather. You listen to them exhaust the options, watching as a second police officer arrives on the other side of the new little river, and you wonder if you could end up spending all night right here in the middle of the backseat with your arm and your knee pressing against Gaspard.

The cars behind you have finally gotten word, and people are turning around or backing carefully off the bridge, returning the way they came. There's nothing to do but wait for the water to go down. Port St. Pete High School is technically a hurricane shelter, and the policeman on your side of the flooded road tells people to go there. You've been in the dingy basement of your school a time or two. It's filled with wrestling mats that smell like rotting sweat. You think about Philippe and Roxanne – the potential convergence. You figure Gaspard will somehow love you back before this is all over.

Gaspard's hands are knotted in his lap, knuckles white. You assume he's never seen this much rain, never taken part in a failed evacuation. We'll pick up the dads then go to the school, Mrs. Eriksson says. Neither of your houses have basements; in fact you're fairly certain there isn't a single house in Port St. Pete with a basement, and most are built on stilts. The only basement you know of is the one at Aunt Louise's house, with a velvet-walled movie room and a mirror-walled exercise studio, neither of which you've seen her use. It is almost half an hour before Mrs. Eriksson is able to turn around and exit the bridge. Her husband and your father are waiting in your father's truck at the other end. They wave and motion her forward, following you back down your street, thick layers of rain obscuring the palm trees and sandy shoulders. Gaspard's knee is still touching yours and you know he must realize it by now. Perhaps he likes the comfort of the small connection. Michael falls asleep beside you, his rhythmic exhalations audible despite the rain. The radio jockey says it's just Roxanne now, that Philippe is all but diminished in her wake. She's swallowed him.

Your mother is on the phone to your aunt. Lou, you must be insane, she says. The storm could make land before we know it – it's best to just sit it out. It will all be fine. Your mother says that last part loudly enough for the ears in the back to hear. It will all be fine. But Aunt Louise is persisting. Your mother turns to Mrs. Eriksson. You won't believe what Lou has done, she says. Aunt Louise is in helicopter. You aren't exactly surprised, and you know your mother isn't either. She gives an exasperated sigh. All this will do is get everyone riled up, she says. Will they even let her land? But Mrs. Eriksson seems relieved and Drew perks up, looking from you to your mother. Have you been in it before, he wants to know. Of course you have. You start to shrug, but don't want to shift the position of your shoulder too much.

Mrs. Eriksson turns the van into the school parking lot and pulls right up to the bus lane in between the main building and the football field. You can see a few other cars. A little huddle of umbrellas is moving up the front steps into the main door, which someone in a poncho – Coach Shapiro, you assume – is holding open. Port St. Pete High accommodates two hundred and seven students, making it the smallest public high school in the state. As old as any structure in town, the school building is a brick box, with a recently added cafeteria wing that smells like fried dough and is never quite full.

The van's headlights are shining onto the football field, illuminating the teal emblem of a manatee emblazoned in a circle at the fifty-yard line. Drew brought Gaspard to a home football game the night after Gaspard arrived. Kinsey Mitchell had not really been your friend since fifth grade, but once she put together the fact that you now lived next door to the French exchange student, she suddenly cared enough to compliment your lip-gloss (you weren't wearing any) and save you a seat on the first row behind the cheerleaders. Gaspard ate a hotdog from the grill run by the Father's Club, and he sat there on the bleachers like the rest of you, leaping to his feet when your running back dove into the end-zone, and yet he was still out of place, a single smooth and delicate macaroon on a plate of Oreos.

The helicopter's massive propeller is barely audible above the sound of the rain. You watch it lower, hovering above the manatee's head, before the wind jerks it backward. It touches down on the tail fin. Most people in Port St. Pete have gone home, consigned to wait out the storm away from windows in their homes, but a few are still in the parking lot, making their way toward Coach Shapiro and the steps down to the old wrestling mats in the basement. Those in the parking lot stop hurrying and stare. You can't make out faces, but you like to think that Kinsey Mitchell is among them. Gaspard is speechless as you all pile out of the car, squinting in the rain. Your father holds Michael, though Michael is much too big to be held, and your mother is still insisting that this isn't necessary as you all jog toward the helicopter's open door. Aunt Louise greets you with a nutty grin, her mop of sandy hair contained only by the thick headset with its attached microphone. She yells out something like *screw you, Roxanne* and dips her head back in a wild laugh.

The seats are situated in three tight rows, the first two facing each other. Your parents and the Erikssons crowd into the first two sets of seats up by the pilot with Aunt Louise, the younger children on their laps. You follow Drew and Gaspard into the back where three tiny seats flip down from the wall. You're in zee middle again, Gaspard says. You shrug. I can trade wiz you. You shake your head, it's fine.

You're sure it's intentional when Gaspard's leg shifts toward yours, your knees reuniting here in a different back seat. This time your skin is damp and they stick a little. Aunt Louise turns around, and you're thankful you can't hear what she's yelling as she nods toward Gaspard and winks at you. The helicopter, as if lifted by a puppeteer in the sky, ascends directly upward, then leans to the left. You can see, over Drew's lap, the roof of your school, then the Exxon station, the Shrimp Shack, and finally the bridge, now deserted save two police cars with their blue lights flashing. Drew is taking pictures on his phone.

After only a few minutes, the rain and the wind are gone, behind you, receding into an unknown blackness that waits for the brunt of the storm. The flight is smooth. Even the loud droning is soothing, a white noise sound machine that makes your eyelids heavy. When the chopper lands in between Aunt Louise's house and barn, you wonder if it wakes up that massive pig. The pilot climbs back to open the door, and you peel your knee away from Gaspard's before he has the chance to do it. It's not raining in Montgomery, and as you file out onto the grass you look up and see a few stars. Aunt Louise is already marching toward her house, which is lit up like a Christmas tree on her otherwise dark expanse of property. She's spewing out orders, who will sleep in which guest rooms. You are in your usual room at the end of the upstairs hallway. It is still painted neon orange, which you picked out when you were little and loved all the more when your mother claimed it burned her eyes.

You all enter through the side door into Aunt Louise's kitchen, which is messy but not dirty. Your mother opens the fridge and hands you a bottle of water, asking you to pass it on. Drew peels a flat cookie from a sheet pan sitting on the stove and asks for the Wi-Fi password. Your mother and Mrs. Eriksson both fuss over Gaspard, touching his shoulders and asking if he needs anything, assuring him this is all very unusual. At least you'll have a great story to tell, your father says to him.

Later in your room, when the knock comes, nearly imperceptible, you feel your pulse in your ears and you realize you were waiting for it. The hallway is dark and it's hard to see him at first. Gaspard makes a face at the neon walls as he comes in and sits on the bed. You sit beside him. Were you scared, you ask Gaspard. Yes, he says. You're paralyzed when you realize for sure that he is leaning towards you. His breath is hot and pungent, and then his mouth presses against yours. It is heavy, wet. Not as you imagined. His tongue – unlike his acrylic cashmere shirt and his macaroon skin – is coarse and reptilian as crosses your lips. He tastes like old Doritos. You break away, leaning back to look at him. You have survived Roxanne and the little river over the bridge, and it was all so much better when it was just a dime-sized patch of your knee pressing against his knee in the dark. You wish you were back in the van, back on the couch watching Gaspard copy your worksheet on the structure of atoms, twirling his stubby pencil through his curls. But now Gaspard is staring at you in the neon room, waiting for what you're going to do next. You press your arm against his arm to see if you can feel it again. You press your knee to his knee. You reach out and touch one of the curls at the base of his neck. His hair feels just the same as your hair. Goodnight, Gaspard, you say.

{ 20 } 1ˢᵗ Place Novel Beginning

Commit No Minor Treason

By Devin Bent

Poppies bloom bright red in the gardens of Gresham, but Elizabeth turns away to examine the stonework in the base of the east tower. The mortar has crumbled for more than two hundred years, and her fingers slip easily between the stones. Once, she fit her fingers and toes into the gaps and climbed to the top – but today she waits at the bottom as the glare of the sun fades the grey stones to white.

The screech of the barn owl sounds above her. "Not at midday," she thinks, and looks up. A window explodes, and her brother Edmund plummets toward her, screaming, haloed by a shimmering cloud of broken glass. He falls at her feet, shards piercing his white flesh, blood pouring from his wounds, his blond head impossibly skewed. Her mother, Lady Longworth, and her sister Anne kneel at his side, weeping. Her father, Lord Longworth, resplendent in scarlet and gold, consoles them. Her uncle Richard is nowhere.

Elizabeth stands in a pool of Edmund's blood; crimson seeps up her trousers. She runs and runs, but her feet churn slowly and the blood creeps higher. "It's not my fault!" she cries. "It's not my fault!"

About the Winners

Devin Bent
1ˢᵗ Place Winner Novel Beginnings
Commit No Minor Treason
75 years old and long retired, I experiment with approaches to sustainable agriculture and animal habitat improvement on our arid acres in the Nambé Badlands.

My writing includes a finished novel, *Commit No Minor Treason*, an unfinished novel, *Pojoaque and the Bomb*, and a short story, 'Holler,' which has been a finalist in two contests. I am the primary author of a short book – *Look Before You Leap . . . into Business* (Pilot Press), and a number of professional articles and papers.

> *"At some point, I discover that I have a bunch of unnecessary pages at the beginning of the novel. I cut them off and write a single one page scene to replace them. This is the genesis of my winning scene in your contest."*

Gary Bolick

3rd Place Winner Creative Non Fiction

Felix and the Silver Surfer

Born and raised in the Winston-Salem/ Clemmons area. Currently live with my wife Jill in Clemmons and two sons: Clint and Ryan. Graduated from Wake Forest and began working any and every type of job that would allow me enough time to write: driving a taxi, waiting tables and my current job, flight attendant.

My first novel, *A Snowman in July* (Creative Arts Publishing) is out of print. My publisher went out of business shortly after *Snowman* was released. I have one novel currently available: *Angel's Oracle* (Penumbra Publishing).

> *"Felix is a composite of several people, to paraphrase Mark Twain, "People I have already met on the river." Each of us, daily, encounters a revelatory moment or person. It is up to the individual to open up and seize that moment or person to effect a change within yourself; let the random school the disciplined."*

Jennifer Bean Bower
1st Place Winner Flash Fiction
Through Time, Tide, and Turmoil
Jennifer Bean Bower is an award-winning writer, native Tar Heel, and graduate of the University of North Carolina at Greensboro. Bower is the author of *North Carolina Aviatrix Viola Gentry: The Flying Cashier*; *Animal Adventures in North Carolina*; *Winston & Salem: Tales of Murder, Mystery and Mayhem*; and *Moravians in North Carolina*. She lives in Winston-Salem, North Carolina, with her husband Larry and their pet rabbit Isabelle.

"My inspiration for the piece came from an actual ballast stone! As I held the stone in my hand, I began to think about its journey through time and the incredible history that must have taken place in its presence. I thought how wonderful it would be if this stone could speak, so I decided to give it a voice."

Susannah Cecil
2nd Place Winner Short Story
Their Crazy

When Susannah Cecil isn't teaching Yoga, Pilates or some such, she writes & folds laundry. She is an alum of Wake Forest University and is a Licensed Professional Counselor. Her writing has been published in *Foliate Oak, MoonShine Review,* & *The Dead Mule School for Southern Literature,* among others. She lives in Clemmons with her family (including a daughter, who knows what it's like to live with boys) & their Jack Russell, Otis.

"The train was approaching full speed, & I had to start writing. Because he wouldn't stop talking, I knew where Jike was going about halfway through the first draft. No time for plotting, that draft was almost complete in one sitting, which is unusual for me. In this case, I found it's true - a character will say what needs to be said if we listen."

<u>Hampton Williams Hofer</u>

3rd Place Winner Short Story

Hurricane Season

Hampton Williams Hofer grew up in Raleigh. She graduated from the University of Virginia with a degree in English Literature, and then spent four years teaching high school in Nashville, TN. She earned an MFA in Creative Writing from New York University's Writer's Workshop in Paris and has recently moved back to Raleigh where she lives with her husband and son.

> *"This story is my first publication! I submitted it in my last week of graduate school, when I realized I better get the ball rolling on being a writer. I got the congratulatory email from Flying South the morning of my MFA graduation, so it was a day of double celebrations."*

Janet Joyner

1st Place Winner Poetry

Breast Stroke

Janet Joyner's poems have appeared in numerous magazines, with prize winning poems honored in the 2011 *Yearbook of the South Carolina Poetry Society*, *Bay Leaves* of the North Carolina Poetry Council in 2010, 2011, and in *Flying South 2014*. Her first collection of poems, *Waterborne*, is the winner of the 2014 Holland Prize and will be published by Logan House Press in the fall.

[The inspiration was] "The painting itself, or more especially, the questions this portrait, extraordinary both in its time and still today, poses around issues of identity, agency, and the dynamics of viewing. How the artist negotiates between private and public, between concealing and revealing, to challenge the genre of demure female portraiture with politically charged subject matter "

Mark Mathosian
2nd Place Winner Creative Non-Fiction
Shock Treatment and the Reluctant Traveler
Mark is a retired financial frauds investigation manager from Florida. He spent most of his working career investigating economic crimes such as mortgage & bank frauds, business opportunity frauds and investment Ponzi schemes. After retiring, he and his wife Kathy moved to Advance, North Carolina to be closer to their grandchildren and to get away from excessive heat and hurricanes. Mark is an accomplished nonfiction writer, book publisher and writing instructor at Salem College, Courses for Community. His hobbies include photographing the moon, collecting meteorites, reading and writing.

"I am an investigator and researcher by nature so I tend to investigate the heck out of any subject I write about. Once I feel comfortable that I have done my homework, I sit down and write the piece. In this case, I mixed my personal experience as a psychiatric aide with research on shock therapy. As a nonfiction writer I find great pleasure when readers learn something new from my work."

Jennie Mejan

2nd Place Winner Poetry,

A Single Page From the History of Hands

Honorable Mention Poetry

Young Cezanne Hears Too Much, Conceives "The Black Clock"

Jennie Mejan's poems have appeared in various publications including *Triggerfish Critical Review* and *The Guardian UK*. She lives in Winston-Salem, NC where she consumes copious amounts of Asian food, piddles in digital collage, and marvels at her children.

> *"Most of my writing happens with my eyes closed. My subject is hiding in the pitch black and I visualize draping the correct words/thoughts over it to expose its most honest form as accurately as possible and with the least gaps between the words. A sort of blindfolded papier-mâché."*

Keith A. Menhinick

1st Place Winner Creative Non Fiction
Altered Mental Status

Keith A. Menhinick is a writer from Hickory, NC. After graduating from Gardner-Webb University, Keith taught High School English and worked at several children's homes. He recently completed his Masters of Divinity at Wake Forest University and now works as a hospital chaplain at Wake Forest Baptist Medical Center. Keith uses the pen to question the intersections of faith and identity, and he explores his passion for music and ritual through his work with his local congregation.

> *"Before I sit down to write, I light a candle. Fire is a ubiquitous symbol in ceremonies throughout the world's religions and cultures. Lighting a candle at my desk reminds me that writing is a holy act of meaning-making and that the divine is present in a particularly heightened way."*

Alice Osborn
Honorable Mention Poetry:
Entreaty to Young Editors

Alice Osborn's past educational and work experience is unusually varied, and it now feeds her work as a poet, as well as an editor-for-hire and popular writing coach. In the past decade, Alice has taught classes and writing workshops to thousands of aspiring authors of nearly all ages from 9 to 90 both around the corner and internationally. *Heroes without Capes* will be her most recent collection of poetry; previous collections are *After the Steaming Stops* and *Unfinished Projects*. Alice is also the editor of the anthologies *Tattoos* and *Creatures of Habitat*, both from Main Street Rag. A North Carolina Writers' Network board member and a Pushcart Prize nominee, her work has appeared in the *News and Observer*, *The Broad River Review*, *The Pedestal Magazine*, *Soundings Review* and in numerous journals and anthologies. When she's not editing or writing, Alice is an Irish dancer, and plays guitar and violin. She lives in Raleigh, North Carolina, with her husband, two children and four very messy and loud birds. Visit Alice's website at www.aliceosborn.com.

"Many of my poems emerge from conflict or trauma. Before I wrote this poem I had recently finished editing a tough manuscript where the writer confused all of their homonyms. That same day happened to be our Third Wed night Open Mic at So & So Books in downtown Raleigh—M. Scott Douglass of Main Street Rag (my publisher) dropped in from Charlotte. Afterwards, as I was relating my traumatic book edit to him, he told me he saw me hitting a big roach with my clipboard during our event (the roach lived). He said, "That's a poem." I carried the roach theme forward, remembering when my

sixth grade teacher told us about his roach whacker—I imme-diately thought of how fixing editing mistakes is a lot like killing roaches. And for the icing: I didn't grow up with roaches, but one of my writing students had—she described what roaches smell like and...the rest is our poem."

W. Scott Thomason
1st Place Winner Short Story
Plywood Jesus

W. Scott Thomason is a native of Winston-Salem, NC. He holds degrees from UNC-Greensboro and an MFA in fiction from McNeese State University (Lake Charles, LA). His fiction has appeared in *Broad River Review*, *The Lindenwood Review*, *The Louisiana Review*, *Roanoke Review*, and *The Sierra-Nevada Review*. He is excited to have a story appear in a journal that doesn't have "review" in the title. He must be some kind of sinner, because he's been exiled to the suburbs of Philadelphia along with his wife and two dogs.

"I don't know a lot about this writing thing, but I do know that a sense of wonder is at the heart of a successful story. I set the story in NC because that's what I know well enough to make it genuine."

DD Upchurch

Honorable Mention Poetry

Elizabethan Sonnet: Heron/Hope

DD Upchurch lives on a pond near Winston-Salem, NC. She graduated from Wake Forest University and studied the history of art at the University of Virginia. Inspired by a recent journey to Kyoto, Japan, she is now writing poems about the Japanese aesthetic of wabi-sabi. "Heron/Hope" is her first sonnet and first submission to a poetry contest.

"A large heron swooped past me so close that I could feel the rush of air from his beating wings. How could it not be a sign?"

Deborah Johnson Wood

3rd Place Poetry

Unquilting Be

Deborah Johnson Wood is a freelance writer and editor in Grand Rapids, MI, where she lives with her husband, Tom. While she loves writing for pay, her passion is playing with words in poetic form. Her poems are often lyrical stories inspired by observations and personal experience. She is an active member of Peninsula Writers, a Michigan-based writers' organization, and is a member of a monthly writers group of poets and novelists.

> *". . . finding the ending? It seemed I didn't know where to stop, how to conclude, or what point I was trying to make. My poetry critique group affirmed the images and emotions I wrote, and nurtured me with their impressions until I could find the ending -- one that transcended the quilt before me and signified another beginning."*